ORDINARY LIFE

ORDINARY
A Memoir
of Illness LIFE

Kathlyn Conway

W. H. Freeman and Company
New York

Interior design by Blake Logan

Library of Congress Cataloging-in-Publication Data

Conway, Kathlyn.
    Ordinary life: a memoir of illness /
    Kathlyn Conway.
       p. cm.
      ISBN 0–7167–3036–7 (hardcover)
      1. Conway, Kathlyn—Health.   2. Cancer—Patients—Biography.
      I. Title.
RC279.6.C66A3   1996
362.1'96994'0092—dc20
[B]
96–273316

                                               CIP

© 1997 by W. H. Freeman and Company

The names of some of the people described in this book have been changed to protect their privacy.

Printed in the United States of America

First printing 1996, RRD

For David, Zach, and Molly

Contents

ORDINARY LIFE

Introduction

I feel like a modern phenomenon—a forty-seven-year-old woman with one husband, two children, and three cancers. It is now over three years since my diagnosis of breast cancer, more than twenty years since a diagnosis of Hodgkin's disease, and nineteen months since a diagnosis of a very early lymphoma. Throughout all this I have maintained that the experience of cancer is without redeeming value; that I have not been transformed by the experience; that it is, beyond all else, a misery to be endured.

From my present vantage point, however, I must admit that I have a more complex view of cancer and personal transformation. I am still convinced that cancer is not transformative, that the trauma did not make me a better person. But I have come to believe that those of us who have been sick do, in myriad ways, transform our experience of illness into something we can manage, into something we can live with, and that this utterly human process is in itself meaningful.

I began to write in an attempt to find my way out of the depression that was the aftermath of my breast cancer. I am a practicing psychotherapist who at the time was resistant to the idea of psychotherapy for myself—perhaps because I had friends to talk to, perhaps because I couldn't admit how out of control I felt, or perhaps because I was filled with self-loathing and expected that soon I would return to my "real self," that the miserable person I had become would recede into the past along with the cancer.

I found that writing provided me with some immediate relief from my depression, that the very act of taking pen to paper was constructive—I was making a story out of this devastating experience of breast cancer, using a creative part of myself, and, in doing so, giving back to myself something that had been lost.

Writing gave me the freedom to be honest in a way that was not always possible in conversation, where, I found, people sometimes cut me off or subtly let me know that they wanted to hear only a particular version of my experience. Some responded by simply telling me other people's cancer stories. It seemed not to matter to them if the stories were relevant to my experience; just the fact that they were about cancer was enough.

The stories others told often seemed to contain a message for me. When I heard the story about an eighty-year-old woman who survived four cancers, I felt that I had better be optimistic and survive. When I heard about a woman who refused chemotherapy for breast cancer but then had a recurrence, I worried about whether I should have chemo as well. When I was told of people who suffered through miserable treatments only to die, I was at a loss as to the point. I realize now that most of the time people had no awareness or intention of upsetting me; they genuinely wanted to offer me encouragement and hope. But they felt compelled to tell me these stories, I think, more for their benefit than for mine—to quell the anxiety they felt. They needed to tell a story, to draw a circle around the threat of cancer, much in the same way that I needed to tell my story.

I wrote voraciously for five months; in the very act of remembering and describing my experience of breast cancer I began to distance myself from the actual illness. I wrote in the present tense as a way to speak from inside the experience, even as the very act of writing placed me outside it. I became the observer as much as the participant.

I created a story that now exists apart from me. It is a story with which I can live. However devastating or overwhelming the experience was, however unflattering I may sometimes have been as a character, the story is manageable. It is confined within the pages of this book, within the contours of the memories I have captured, within the limits of my ability to understand. This is the story I will carry with me.

In writing about my breast cancer I also wrote about my experience of Hodgkin's disease. That story took shape when, as a twenty-six-year-old graduate student, I tried to tame my fear by telling everyone I met, even complete strangers, the details of my radiation treatments. The diagnosis had been devastating, at the time unlike anything in my experience or that of my friends. I was at the beginning of a blossoming relationship and a promising career. I wanted to have children. I was shattered by the loss of possibility, the loss of my future. Through the years, I refined the story, and what I now remember, with rare exception, seems limited to the tales I came to repeat.

With time, the statistical probability that I was cured seemed confirmed, and I came to feel that my Hodgkin's disease was behind me. I had moved on to my life, career, and family. In retrospect, it had become an acute episode, a nightmare that had faded from my everyday awareness.

When I was diagnosed with first-stage breast cancer at forty-three, such horrors were no longer unique among my peers. I wasn't special this time. I knew many women with breast cancer, and certainly most of my friends were no longer strangers to medical crises. But, ironically, this commonality of experience did not spare me the abject loneliness of cancer, for which, it seems, there's little comfort in community. Nor did the fact of my having had cancer before make it any easier; it's not something you get better at. My diagnosis and what ensued pulled me into the closed circle of fear in which I had lived when I had Hodgkin's disease, except to this was added the responsibility of being a parent.

In December 1994, evidence of a third cancer was found, a lymphoma for which my doctors did not recommend treatment, because there was no sign of cancer beyond some scattered cells in a node that had been removed from my clavicle. My doctors have followed me closely with tests and CAT scans, and as of July 1996 no further evidence of lymphoma has been found. If it had, I would need a new story to tell myself. In that story, the experience of my first two cancers would undoubtedly take a different shape.

Certainly the details of that story would be important—what happened to my body, how I felt and thought about it, how people responded to me. But the ability to tell a story would be equally important, as a way to make sense, at least within my narrative, of another chaotic episode in my life. Although the story would not redeem the experience, it would help to restore me to myself.

Since completing chemotherapy, I've spoken with many women undergoing chemo. Throughout my own treatment I struggled with the feeling that I was a worse patient than anyone else—more nauseated, more cranky, more self-absorbed. In speaking with these women, I discovered how similar our experiences were: we all went through the shock of diagnosis, the fear of treatment, the struggle to manage our lives, the difficulties with the responses of our family, friends, and doctors, the profound loneliness.

At the same time, each woman's story was completely different, depending on the circumstances of her life. One woman was trying to become pregnant and faced the loss of that possibility; a second was the mother of four young children, struggling with the daily problems of arranging babysitting and finding the strength to get to her treatments on public transportation; a third was single and looking for support among her friends; a fourth was widowed and trying to manage her treatments while remaining independent, so as not to burden her adult children.

And each woman's response to her cancer was different. One woman cried all the time, finding some relief in her tears; another never cried, rarely complained, and talked only about how she was doing well and would be fine. One woman dropped out of her professional life for a while and focused all her resources on getting better; another preferred company, support groups, lots of contact with people. One woman was furious all the time, whereas another seemed resigned to her fate. One found comfort in religion, another in music and reading; a third could find no comfort.

What struck me was how mesmerized I was by each story. Each had its own integrity, its own shape, detail, humor, and pain. I see now that I was caught up with each woman as she, in speaking, began to make something unique out of her struggles. Each was beginning to create the story that would delineate her experience of breast cancer, contain it, and ultimately give her some distance from it—enabling her to accept it as her own.

I offer my story.

Chapter one

Waiting Rooms

It is March 31, 1993, two years since my last mammogram and the day I am scheduled for another. Because the *New York Times* has been filled with the controversy over whether mammograms are of value to women in their forties and because I am forty-three, I have been uncertain about whether to proceed with this test. In checking with my friends who are doctors, I learn that mammograms often produce false positives and sometimes cannot detect tumors that are present. Nor do they seem to improve the statistical survival rates of women in their forties, according to some studies. So why expose us to even the low doses of radiationfrom mammograms or to the possibility of unnecessary biopsies? I call Dr. Balick, my gynecologist, who understands my dilemma but feels that, given my history of Hodgkin's disease, I should proceed with the screening test. I take his advice, perhaps because I tend to do what I have been told to do by someone in authority, but largely because I will never forgive myself if I choose not to have the test and then later discover that I missed a problem.

I go to the lab on Park Avenue only to learn that it has relocated several blocks farther downtown. I run there so as not to be late. The office is crowded with people waiting, looking bored or worried. When the technician calls me in, I talk with her about the controversy regarding mammograms. She's angry about the recent publicity given to studies that indicate no increase in survival rates for women in their forties who have mammograms. She has seen so many women who discovered a cancer early through a mammogram. Of course, I think, an x-ray technician would believe in the efficacy of x-rays. I feel I am having an unnecessary test for which I have no time. I undress and put on a gown. The technician places my breast between two plates and then turns the knob until the plates squeeze my breast tightly. It hurts. The machine is like a medieval instrument of torture. The technician arranges my other breast, takes more x-rays, and then tells me to wait while she checks the films.

Ten minutes later she returns. She would like to take a few more x-rays, she says. I ask if there's something wrong. She evades my question, saying only that she needs a clearer picture of my left breast. I feel my heart pound. The additional x-rays take some time because the technician is trying to position me in just the right way to get a good picture of something. I'm screaming in my head for David.

I walk almost mechanically to the reception area and wait for the x-ray films to take to my gynecologist. The technicians and receptionists chatting together behind the desk now seem cruel and indifferent. I'm panic-stricken, and they are acting as if life is carefree. I focus all my rage on them. When the technician hands me the x-rays, she says only that the report will be sent to my doctor. I know not to ask what she's seen or show my terror, because she's not allowed to tell me anything.

I hail a cab that takes me up Park Avenue and over to the West Side. In the back seat I slip the films out of the manila envelope and examine the half spheres that represent my breasts, each comprising light and dark areas with faint, silken threads running through them, all in magnetic black and silver tones so unlike my body's colors. I have no idea how to read them, but I focus on some large, white dots and try, without success, to wrench some meaning from them. Panic rises in me. I tell myself that it may be nothing, yet I feel that something is wrong. My body is numb; it cannot be true.

When I enter our apartment on Riverside Drive, I'm relieved to hear David working at his computer. I stand next to his desk, my body rigid, and tell him that they have found something on my mammogram. I see a flash of terror in his eyes, but he quickly invites me with his arms and lets me collapse into him. We've been at this juncture before. When I was twenty-six and a graduate student at Harvard I was told that I had Hodgkin's disease. I walked back to David's apartment from the university clinic in a state of shock. I met him outside fixing his car. We seemed to collapse into each other then, to hold each other up as we walked to his apartment. I don't remember the time immediately after that. Just the collapse. This collapse. That collapse. I cry. He struggles to pull himself together so that he can mobilize us for the days ahead. I put in a call to Dr. Balick. I try to calm myself, to remember that this is not a diagnosis of a new cancer, at least not yet. But, having had cancer once, it feels like I am back in a dark, cold place— the bottom of a deep well where the light of my daily life cannot reach me. No one can rescue me, nor can I escape. I can feel no hope in this place, only dread of an illness that may take my life, and fear of all that can happen to me against my will.

All evening I am in a stupor as I go through the motions of preparing dinner, folding clothes, and returning phone calls. Zach, who is eleven, needs me to look over his homework, and Molly, who is seven, wants me to read to her. When Dr. Balick returns my call, I leave Molly with David and go to another phone so that she will not hear. Dr. Balick had called the lab to get the mammogram report by phone. They found "suspicious calcifications" in my left breast, he explains. He's already called his colleague Dr. Cody, a breast surgeon, who says that 75 percent of the time these calcifications are benign but that it will probably be necessary to do a biopsy. Dr. Cody can fit me in tomorrow if I call in the morning to make an appointment. Dr. Balick assures me that I will be in good hands and that, if it is breast cancer, we seem to have caught it early. I try to sound reasonable and refrain from screaming at him that he must not mention cancer. He really trusts Dr. Cody's knowledge and knows that he will not do unnecessary procedures. If he had a wife who needed a biopsy, this is the surgeon he would recommend. I wonder why this "if I had a wife" reassurance is supposed to work.

I thank him for his quick response and referral to Dr. Cody. We joke a little—he about Dr. Cody's name, Hiram Cody, III, nicknamed Chip, and about how tall Dr. Cody is, towering over him on the tennis court. I assure Dr. Balick that he has now redeemed himself for having nearly missed Molly's birth, despite his promise to be present for the labor and delivery.

Inside my head, however, I'm going crazy. This phone call makes the problem in my breast real. Whatever distance I had been able to place between myself and the possibility of breast cancer is gone. I feel flushed; my heart is pounding and my breath is short. I cannot organize myself to prepare coffee, make the kids' lunches, and check to see if they've packed their homework and brushed their teeth. My mind goes over and over what Dr. Balick said— that 75 percent of the time these calcifications are nothing. So 25 percent of the time they are cancer. My thoughts race past too fast to sort out. This could be the beginning of a nightmare. I may actually have breast cancer. My God, no. My kids. This can't be true. What do I need to do right now? Who will meet Molly after school tomorrow? Is

Dr. Cody the right doctor? How will I get through the night? What if I'm forced to give my parents bad news? What are Molly and Zach doing now?

For brief periods in the evening, I slow myself down enough to be reasonable, to say to myself that there's probably nothing wrong, that this is just a terrible scare. When I speak to my friend Bonnie, I talk as if I am most upset that I will take my worry on vacation. David and I have planned a week's trip to Washington, D.C., with Zach and Molly, and we've anticipated this time together with great enthusiasm. The impending biopsy is merely a nuisance that could have been avoided had I not scheduled the mammogram for today.

David and I settle Molly and Zach into bed and we talk. What about this breast surgeon? Should I go to him? Is he the best? We joke about who goes to the doctors who aren't the best. Should we check with our friends in the medical world for the "perfect" surgeon? Will I need a second opinion? Am I overreacting? We look up Dr. Cody's name in the phone book. He lives in our neighborhood—somehow that's comforting. He has an office near New York Hospital and Memorial Sloan-Kettering Cancer Center, so Dr. Balick must be right about his competence. I feel reassured enough to proceed with the consultation and then make a decision about the surgeon.

回

My appointment the next day is for 2:45 PM. Molly generally spends her afternoons with me, so I arrange for her to go home with a friend after school. Zach plays basketball at the 92nd Street Y on Thursdays. David clears his schedule so that he can go with me. Since my work as a psychotherapist is done in an office in our apartment, I am able to see patients in the morning, almost forgetting what awaits me in the afternoon.

Because it is raining and windy, David and I take a cab to the East Sixties, arrive early, and search for a coffee shop. Finally, we discover a rather elegant place where David orders a salad, I some chamomile tea and a muffin. I am distracted and afraid. I resent the other customers, some in mink coats, leisurely drinking coffee, oblivious, and seeming so relaxed. David and I talk about my fear of having cancer again and about our concern for the kids. I try to imagine my meeting with Dr. Cody. I wonder what he is like. David reminds me of the likelihood that I will need a biopsy and that this appointment today will probably not provide me with resolution. We proceed four blocks uptown to Dr. Cody's office on East Sixty-eighth Street. A narrow path flanked by low evergreen shrubs leads to a modern building. The office is on the first floor at the left. We enter a long narrow room where no one else is waiting.

I wonder at the number of chairs. Why would so many women ever be waiting to see a breast surgeon? I check in with the receptionist and sit down next to David. He takes my hand in his. I stare straight ahead, as if by holding still I can stop time. I cannot speak, but David's hand keeps me grounded.

This appointment must be what a blind date feels like—waiting for this man I've never met, hoping we will get along, wondering whether I will trust him. But why do I think of a date? A date would certainly hold some eager anticipation, whereas the prospect of this meeting seems thoroughly gruesome. But it is about my body, about something intimate that might happen with this stranger. I am about to meet the man I may choose to cut into my breast. Yesterday I could not have imagined this meeting. I planned only to be packing for our trip to Washington.

The receptionist calls my name and ushers David and me into the office. Dr. Cody certainly is tall. He is fair and wears a bow tie. He's younger than I and Protestant, I assume. Last cancer, I trusted my life to Dr. Rosenthal, who was of medium height, dark, Jewish, and older than I, though young himself at the time. Dr. Cody is warm and professional as he shakes our hands. It's all right now. This man may help me.

Dr. Cody asks about my family's medical history. I am relieved to focus on this concrete recitation of facts; it helps me hold on to who I am. I tell him that, though there is heart disease in my family, there has been no one with cancer except me. I mention that my sister Chris was recently diagnosed with Budd-Chiari disease, a blood-clotting disorder that causes liver damage. Dr. Cody takes my medical history, posing questions that indicate he is knowledgeable about Hodgkin's disease, a cancer of the lymph system. I tell him that my Hodgkin's disease was diagnosed from an enlarged node above my collarbone on my left side. I was treated at Peter Bent Brigham Hospital in Boston. At that time the doctors removed my spleen in order to check for cancer cells. They also performed a laparotomy, an abdominal surgery during which they biopsied various lymph nodes and organs. Because no further cancer was found, they determined that I had first-stage Hodgkin's disease.

I answer more questions, telling him I received radiation treatments in the area surrounding the original node and in the mediastinum—part of the chest area. He nods knowingly and asks if I've had any problems since then. Not until now, I say, except the loss of hearing in my left ear. He asks about my menstrual history and takes down the history of my pregnancies. In addition to having two children, I've had one miscarriage. Have I ever taken birth control pills? Once, for a few months. Any difficulty with my breasts, any swelling, discomfort, lumps? No.

As he records this information, my eyes roam around the room. I notice his diplomas from Dartmouth College and Columbia University medical school. His credentials put me at ease, but I'm not sure about the bow tie. On his wall is a painting of a man who I imagine is his father, perhaps the other doctor named Cody whom we found in the phone book. I'm glad he has a father. Does he have children? I want him to know that what matters most about possibly having breast cancer is that I am part of a family. I have parents, a husband, and children.

He places my x-rays on a back-lit screen for us to see. He points out the calcifications in the left breast. David and I realize that we had not even seen this cluster of small dots. We thought the culprits were the three large, white dots that turn out to be of no significance. So much for our diagnostic skills. Given their size and the way the dots line up, Dr. Cody thinks that the calcifications are small and within the duct.

He bends over his desk and draws a picture of how he imagines these calcifications. He explains that he will need to do what is called a wire localization biopsy. First, a technician will insert a wire into the area of the breast where the x-rays indicate the calcifications are located. During surgery, Dr. Cody will remove the lump and a small margin of tissue surrounding it. He will immediately send it to the lab to determine whether it is benign or cancerous, and he will be able to tell me right after the biopsy. If the tumor is cancerous, he will know from the biopsy whether it has penetrated the duct. It is likely that he will need to go in another time and do a lumpectomy—that is, cut out more breast tissue—to be sure that he's left a margin of healthy tissue surrounding the area where the lump had been. This would provide some assurance that he'd removed all of the tumor. He explains that a lumpectomy is typically followed by radiation in an attempt to rid the area of any remaining cancer cells. Because of my medical history, however, radiation might not be advisable and he might need to do a mastectomy, that is remove the entire breast; but for now we need to focus on the biopsy. Although I hear mention of a mastectomy, the thought is too monstrous for me to consider right now. Besides, I may not even have cancer.

He tells me that he would like to examine me. It's amazing how quickly I withdraw all emotional significance from my breasts so that I can let him examine them. These breasts are no longer breasts that give sexual pleasure, nor are they breasts for nursing. They've become mere appendages, parts of my body to be examined and felt for tumors. They are suspect, perhaps guilty. He examines each breast and finds no palpable lump. He feels the lymph nodes under each of my arms and I notice myself tense up. Because of my Hodgkin's disease, lymph nodes always worry me, and so I'm relieved when he finds nothing suspicious there. Dr. Cody assures me that the biopsy can safely wait a week and suggests that David and I go ahead and enjoy our vacation.

Relaxing with my family no longer seems a possibility, but we decide to go anyway because I have canceled sessions with my patients and the children have vacation from school. I suggest that we cut our trip short and schedule surgery later the following week. We settle on Thursday, and because we plan to leave tomorrow, Dr. Cody suggests that I have the pre-operation tests done at New York Hospital this afternoon. He shakes our hands and leaves the office with us so that he can speak to the secretary about arranging the tests. As I leave, I am thinking that I like him a lot but want him to know something about me, about who I am and what I do. Maybe then I would feel less like a ghost of myself. And, because my life is on the line, I'd like him to know something about that life. But his time is precious, I realize, and he has been very generous with it.

We leave the office and I begin to cry. I keep repeating to David that this can't be happening to me. I've already had my turn with cancer. I never imagined that I could get another cancer years later. Great denial, I am thinking. I love my life, my family, my work. I don't want all this to be threatened. David's arm is around me and he stops to hug me as we walk down the block. We agree that this is a doctor we can trust. David is clearly impressed with his knowledge and his willingness to explain procedures carefully and answer our questions. I, however, though now comfortable with Dr. Cody, work over in my mind the nightmarish possibilities—malignancy, more surgery, radiation.

We wend our way through the construction barriers outside the entrance to New York Hospital. It is already four o'clock. I find a phone to call the mother of Molly's friend to ask if Molly can stay longer. We seldom change plans like this, and Molly will be upset. I speak to her briefly on the phone and give her a sense of when we will return and what the evening will be like. David and I realize that we can pick Zach up at the Y later as planned.

We follow the signs to the waiting room for the pre-op tests. The secretaries look efficient as they walk back and forth behind the front desk, friendly with each other and perfunctory with me as they hand me some papers. I fill out the medical history form, which contains the same questions I was asked by Dr. Cody. I know this is only the beginning. Why not hand out a standard form that could be completed and taken from doctor to doctor? Perhaps they'd like to hire me to organize this place. I list my surgeries, and I note that I am allergic to cortisone taken internally, an odd allergy that medical personnel always question. Person to contact in case of death. Oh, great. It is only twenty-four hours since my mammogram and I am sitting in a hospital contemplating the possibility of my death.

David and I are a little giddy—perhaps relieved about Dr. Cody, perhaps grateful for being hustled quickly through this process, perhaps hysterical. I am first directed to the billing office where, I assume, they will verify that I have insurance before I have any tests. A tall, well-dressed woman sitting at her computer in the small office does not look up when we enter but tells us to be seated. We sit and watch as she finishes some typing and files some papers. Eventually she looks up and formally introduces herself. She remains distant and professional as she takes down extensive information from us. Finally, when she realizes that I am adequately insured and thus will not cause her problems, her demeanor completely changes; she becomes warm and friendly and her body relaxes. We must call the insurance company to get preapproval for the surgery, she tells us. By the end of the interview she is positively talkative, chatting with David about Baruch College, where he teaches history, and with me about my psychotherapy practice. David and I laugh as we leave, amused by the radical personality change we have just witnessed.

When I return to the pre-op area, I am ushered into another waiting room and given a gown, bathrobe, and slippers to put on. It's cold here. I wait with two other women. I smile but it's obvious that neither wishes to make contact with me. An older man comes in to wait. He tells me that he is having surgery and he looks worried. He wants to be home in time to celebrate Passover with his family but is afraid that it is unlikely. His seder and my vacation are events of little consequence to this hospital, where the scheduling of medical procedures and surgeries takes precedence over anything else in our lives.

Eventually I am called for an EKG. The technician is pleasant but does not respond to my periodic attempts at conversation. Why won't she talk to me about what's happening? I assume she would rather not hear my worries. I lie on the table and she applies cream to various spots on my torso and then little rubber suction cups connected by wires to a machine. The machine will record electrical impulses and assure me that all is well with my heart.

At least I hope it will reassure me. I look at the photos of this woman's daughter on the wall. It's the end of the day and I'm sure she wants to hurry to see her. This is her job. It's routine for her. I want to get home to my daughter, too, and to my son. But the hospital personnel don't seem to care about that really. I am just a body, at their disposal for as long as it takes them.

Next, I'm sent down the hall for a chest x-ray. This technician is an awkward, scowling, unattractive man. I don't think about his life, because I imagine he doesn't have much of one, and it's clear that he doesn't want to converse. Like that for the mammogram, this procedure seems like something out of a back ward of the 1950s. He slides large metal plates in and out of the machine, tells me where to place my arms, turns me this way and that. He leaves the room to push the remote button for the x-ray. I am alone. He goes outside to protect himself from the radiation. I have no protection. In fact, I must assume that the radiation he avoids will help me.

Now I can dress again. Keep moving. Act normal. I join David in the waiting room and we talk about plans for the evening. We will have to explain to Molly and Zach that I saw the doctor and will need more tests after vacation, just to be sure everything is okay. I find myself pushing aside the horror of what I might have to tell them. What should we do for dinner? We decide to order from the Cuban-Chinese restaurant at our corner and have it delivered.

I'm called again, this time to the lab where I'm handed a cup for urine. I go into the bathroom and read the instructions for obtaining a sample. Such sanitized language. When I emerge, I'm ushered into a chair with a side table, reminiscent of Mrs. Miller's fourth grade classroom. I place my arm on the table so that the nurse can take my blood. She engages in animated and intelligent conversation with another nurse while she works on me. Although I mind being ignored, it's some consolation to find the conversation interesting. As my blood is drawn, I remember the irony of receiving in the mail a request that I donate blood when I had Hodgkin's disease. If only I could have donated then. If only I could now.

We take a cab to the 92nd Street Y to pick up Zach. We tell him only that I will need to have some tests next week, that the doctor saw something on the x-ray of my breast and needs to check it out. "But you'll be all right?" Zach asks. "Yes," I find myself saying. He's in a great mood and seems to accept the news in the matter-of-fact way we have presented it to him. Later, at home, Molly reacts similarly. Thank God they don't understand what this could mean. Our evening is focused on preparing for our trip. As I pack, my mind roams from thoughts of toothbrushes, shampoo, and underwear to cancer, suffering, death.

⊡

On Friday David brings home our new Toyota minivan. He's proud of the good deal he made after endless days of bargaining with car dealers. Until yesterday I enjoyed listening to his tales, but now, by numbing myself to fear, I have managed to quell any excitement I've had about the van or the trip. We pick the kids up after school and give them a first ride through Central Park so that they can explore the van. I sit stonily in the front seat, unmoved by the bright day, the glistening park, the majestic apartment buildings at its edge. Why, when I have so much—this family, this life—do I insist on acting morose? This is only a biopsy. David puts on a compact disk of Eric Clapton singing "Tears in Heaven," the song he wrote for his toddler son who died after falling from their apartment window. How did he ever write that song?

In the evening David's brother, his sister, and her sons join us for dinner to welcome home David's parents, Alex and Sophie, who have spent the winter in Florida. We enjoy a comfortable evening together, everyone vying to talk, Alex and Sophie relating tales of their trip with periodic wrangling over details. Although they had a terrific time, they are as thrilled to be home with us as we are to have them back. We order a large container of spaghetti and meatballs from Carmine's and celebrate all the birthdays of the past month—Molly's, Zach's, David's, Alex's. Molly and Zach relish the love, attention, and presents heaped on them by their grandparents. I tell David's sister, Adrienne, about my scheduled biopsy, and she assures me I will be fine. None of us can really allow for a worse possibility.

The next morning we set off on our Washington trip. David has worked incredibly hard all year teaching and writing and I have been busy with my practice. For months we've looked forward to this time with each other and with our kids, but now I resent the pressure of having to hide my feelings, and I fear a vacation of restless nights followed by mornings when I wake to the jolting thought of what may lie ahead. Perhaps we should have canceled the trip, but how could we disappoint Molly and Zach? Besides, we would need to occupy them for a week at home anyway.

The kids each have their own row in the van, equipped with a tape player and headphones. As David and I talk in the front seat, he puts his hand on mine. We drive south through the Amish country—beautiful farmland dotted with houses that have no electricity. We stop at the visitors' center in a small town where we watch a film about Amish life. David whispers in my ear, "What do they do for medical care?" I love quilts but can't focus on the beautiful array displayed in the store down the block. Instead I am reminded of the nine-patch quilt I made during my radiation treatments, sewing small squares together by hand and feeling some small pleasure in the colors, the pattern, the productivity. I have a number of quilts, discovered in small antique shops over the years. Why do I think only of the one connected to my Hodgkin's disease? Why does my mind keep returning to memories of that experience, long tucked away before this week? It's as if the threat of a new cancer has placed me on a vast and desolate plain where spotlights illuminate only the old painful experiences and darkness blankets all good memories and all that gives me joy in my everyday life.

As we drive on to Hershey, Pennsylvania, we eat oranges and I read a brochure describing a ten-minute tour of the chocolate factory. This will not be Willy Wonka's, but we decide the kids will like it. We park in a gigantic lot and enter the "factory" with hundreds of other tourists. This is certainly not the tour that David nostalgically recalls from his childhood. Like parts on an assembly line, we are moved past displays of the production process. My thoughts go from the chocolate factory to the factory-like hospital to surgery to cancer.

At Gettysburg we check into a hotel across from the rooming house where Lincoln stayed. Molly and Zach are fascinated by the fact that the TV in our room is hidden in a cabinet with doors that close. We tour the historic houses of the town, I in a daze and unable to react. David, Zach, and Molly, interested in the information provided by the guide, are animated and seemingly oblivious to my private sadness. In the evening we order pizza for the kids and sit them happily in front of a movie. This arrangement is a first, and David and I take advantage of it to go downstairs to the restaurant. I now feel more relaxed and talkative, musing to David about how I couldn't possibly have cancer when I feel so healthy.

The next day we drive to the battlefields. I notice the pit in my stomach again and realize that the thin veil that generally keeps me from knowledge of my mortality has been torn away. I can think only about dying. An ordinary day as a tourist takes on a bittersweet quality. At the information center we hear an account of the battle. Luckily, I am annoyed enough at the presentation to concentrate more on the Civil War than on cancer for a few minutes. Military strategy is interesting, but this was a war about slavery and there's no mention of it. Perhaps they don't want to offend visitors whose relatives were Confederate soldiers; but they're alienating us instead. We do a lot of explaining to the kids.

We visit the cemetery, probably not a good place for me right now. Zach and Molly read us the Gettysburg Address from a plaque mounted there and then run among the gravestones. We hire a guide who drives us through the battlefields for two hours. I am grateful to this man who thoroughly engages my interest in events outside myself. He shows us the huge cannons and describes the psychology of the battle formations. Soldiers marched shoulder to shoulder, insuring that those in command could easily spot men fleeing the line and shoot them. Before a battle, the infantrymen were stationed behind embankments, so they could not see the open field onto which they were about to march. Would they have charged had they known what easy targets they would become? As with surgery, it is sometimes better not to know what lies ahead.

We proceed to Washington, too early for the cherry blossoms. The gray March day reflects my mood. As we walk about the city, I am short-tempered with the kids, bothered by their running and jumping, the expression of their liveliness. Do I want them to act as frozen as I feel? I'm irritated with myself for not relaxing and enjoying their company. David manages to be involved with them, as always. Why am I angry rather than grateful to him?

Because he is not as morose as I? Because I have been robbed of my ease with my children and envy his ability to stay connected to them?

We visit the planetarium, where the show about the planets becomes a Rorschach test for me. I see only breasts with dots on them; calcifications, I imagine. The children jog on the mall. Molly beams with pride about the distance she runs, and Zach takes on the role of coach, which allows him to race about like the boy he's beginning to outgrow. At the Lincoln Memorial, David recalls the many demonstrations he participated in here; I'm preoccupied with the thought that I'll never visit this place again without recalling not the excitement of antiwar marches but this day of thinking about breast cancer and feeling estranged from my own children.

The drive home is difficult. The last time I had a biopsy the tumor was cancerous—Hodgkin's disease. I was twenty-six and coming back from my spring vacation to have Dr. McKittrick biopsy the lump on my neck. The expected twenty-minute surgery lasted two and a half hours. Because I was given only a local anesthetic, I was aware of everything—the doctor pulling at things in my neck, working hard to find the lump and remove it, sewing up tissue, fat, and skin. During the operation I kept insisting that I would faint. The nurse, who, like me, grew up in Buffalo, assured me that I could not faint while lying down. She skillfully talked me through the surgery.

We left, suspecting nothing, and we failed to grasp the import of her statement to David that I would need a lot of tender, loving care. I hope that this time is different and that in a week I am one of those women who resents mammograms for causing unnecessary biopsies. But I have never been known to look on the bright side of things.

When the Manhattan skyline comes into view, I'm seized by an unbearable sense of dread. I would do anything to stop all that is happening to me. I think of all the bargains with God that David and I have been proposing. He'll give up tenure, our house in the country, even our New York apartment in exchange for my health. I'll join the Peace Corps, adopt some homeless children. The thought of abandoned children makes me think of Molly and Zach. I cry silently in the front seat but then realize that Zach notices I'm upset. "Everything will be fine," I tell him; "I'm just a little nervous." How can he believe that I'm fine if I'm crying all the time? Why can't I hide my feelings better?

On Thursday morning David and I rise early. We've left Molly and Zach with David's parents to spend the night. I put on comfortable clothes but no make-up. I am not allowed to eat or drink anything. We go out into the early morning light and walk down the block to our car. I remember having watched Ed, our friend and neighbor, walk down this block a few years ago on his way to the exploratory surgery in which they found the rampant cancer that soon killed him. I sit very still and silent in the front seat. David squeezes my hand. I know he cannot stand that I am in such pain.

We park the car and find our way to the outpatient surgery waiting room. Even at seven in the morning many patients are already there, dressed in bathrobes and sitting with their relatives and friends. It's like prison—the clothes signal who is being punished and who is visiting. I notice once again how little interest the staff has in the patients. We are a job to them. If they were to make contact with us, they might know that we are frightened and would have to talk to us; they could not move us through so efficiently. I see a woman my age sitting between her husband and her mother, who looks particularly distraught. The woman herself appears relaxed, certainly not how I must appear. Finally I'm given a hospital gown, a robe, and slippers and taken to a changing room. The nurse gives me a key to the locker where I can leave my clothes. There I meet a younger woman, and we exchange comments about our nervousness and wonder together whether the gown opens in the front or back.

In the waiting room David, who has written a history of nineteenth-century hospitals, launches into a critique of hospital policy. To save money patients are admitted the morning of surgery, not the night before. This giant waiting room cuts down on personnel and therefore on financial costs. But not on human costs, I think. Dr. Cody comes in to talk to the woman I have been watching, his first patient. He bends his tall frame and speaks to her warmly. I am reminded of what a kind man he seems to be. He also greets us and tells us it will be a few hours. David and I sit and wait, trying to read and look nonchalant in this room filled with people all trying to look unconcerned. Every so often I mumble to David that I can't stand this; I can't do it.

A nurse finally calls my name and brings a wheelchair. She takes me up in the elevator, then down a hall to a room where I meet the radiology technician, the first staff member to talk to me like a real person. She tells me she knows how difficult this experience is and promises to make it as comfortable as possible. She explains that it's necessary to take some x-rays of my breast, which will guide her to the exact location of the calcifications. She will give me a local anesthetic and then insert a small needle into my breast, pointing toward the calcifications. Through the needle she will insert a wire with a hook on the end and position it where the calcifications are located. The wire will remain in place during the surgery to indicate their site to the surgeon.

She seats me in a chair and proceeds with the x-rays. After viewing them, she does the procedure, talking calmly as she works, as if this is a normal event. Soon the radiologist, a young doctor, comes in and looks at the "pictures." Why is he male and she female, he white and she black? Why will he get paid much more for this two-minute visit than she for all her time, skill, and kindness?

The radiologist casually compliments me for not fainting and describes how anxious women often are during this procedure. I'm momentarily flattered by his comments, but I remind myself not to give these performance evaluations too much weight; I may not always do so well. Dr. Cody arrives to check the x-rays, and I wait for him in the wheelchair in the hall, where I can look out over the East River. He comes and sits on the windowsill near me.

He notices that, in fact, I don't feel so brave at all. He tries to calm me by going over the possibilities and assuring me that, even if he finds something, he will be able to treat it. I listen but say little.

On the way to the elevator we joke about the absurdity of his wheeling me when I am perfectly capable of walking. As we wait for the elevator, a pretty young woman in a hospital gown approaches me, smiling. I'm startled to realize that she is one of my patients. I knew she was having a lymph node biopsied this week to see if she has Hodgkin's disease, but at this exact time, in this hospital? To calm her fears, I had shared with her my own experience, offering myself as an example of how one can be healthy seventeen years after Hodgkin's disease. So much for that, I think, as I sit in this wheelchair, feeling small and vulnerable, introducing her to Dr. Cody and to the possibility that I am not so unscathed. She thought I was on vacation, she says. I explain that I'm having a biopsy to check out something that showed up on my mammogram and I ask how she's doing. I'll speak to her later. In the elevator I laugh to myself that this is a patient's worst nightmare, and a therapist's. To think that I and my patients have been bothered by running into each other on weekends while doing errands.

Dr. Cody leaves me outside the operating room while he goes to prepare for surgery. At twenty-six I was anesthetized before being wheeled to surgery, so I've never really seen a big operating room. Where are the bright lights and the activity promised me by TV's hospital dramas? I see only a solitary woman swabbing the floor. This certainly takes the magic out of sterilization: it's just like mopping my kitchen floor. The room is full of glistening, stainless steel. I think of all the women I have known who have had biopsies and how little thought I have given to what was entailed. I always imagined some quick office procedure, not surgery. An anesthesiology resident asks me the usual presurgery questions. He has a lousy bedside manner. I feel exposed and foolish. I think of my children. Maybe in a few hours this will seem like a bad dream.

The resident takes me into the operating room, helps me onto the table and introduces the anesthesiologist. Dr. Cody washes his hands while the nurses set up instruments and supplies. I'm surprised at how many people this procedure requires, but at least this bustle of doctors and nurses lives up to my TV version of "real" surgery. Because the resident has failed to find my vein despite numerous jabs at my arm, the anesthesiologist takes over and inserts the IV needle. He explains that he will give me some medication to make me drowsy. I will not be completely asleep but will feel as though I am floating. I will feel no pain. People in surgical gowns begin to gather around me. Dr. Cody stands over me and says not to worry: the anesthesia will last for the length of the surgery and I will wake up in the recovery room. He will meet me there and we will talk.

During surgery I feel a pleasant sensation, definitely like floating, just as I was told. I feel like an astronaut in an enclosed space, warmer than I imagine a space capsule—womb-like, in fact, which may account for the good and safe feeling. The faces of the doctors and nurses operating on me seem large and close, more cartoonlike than threatening. Although I am vaguely aware of their activity in my body, I feel no embarrassment or even annoyance at their intrusion, and I'm not in pain. At some point I notice the doctors and nurses putting things away, as if they're closing up shop.

I wake up in a big, bright room. Other patients, all women, sit in chairs facing the window while nurses bustle about. When David comes in, he looks very concerned. I tell him that I think Dr. Cody found something. Soon Dr. Cody himself arrives. We again sit near a window, he on the windowsill, David and I on chairs. He tells us that he found a small tumor and sent the specimen to the lab, where it was determined to be malignant. In his opinion, it is a "garden variety" breast cancer; although it has penetrated the duct, it seems to be small and localized.

Dr. Cody continues to talk, more to David, it seems, than to me. I'm in shock but still groggy from the anesthesia. I feel David's arm around me and trust that he's following what Dr. Cody is saying. I focus all my energy on holding myself together. I need to get out of here so that I can sob in private. On his surgical gown, on his knee, Dr. Cody draws a picture of a small oblong tumor and explains where it was located in my breast. For this tumor he would normally recommend a lumpectomy during which he would remove a wider area of tissue, followed by radiation treatments of the area where the tumor was, but, as he mentioned before, it might not be advisable for me to have radiation again in that area. He needs to look at my records and consult with some radiologists. If radiation is not possible, we will have to consider a mastectomy and chemotherapy. We should go home and rest and come to his office Tuesday, when he will have the pathology report.

David tries to calm me as he leads me outside, repeating whatever hopeful information he gleaned from Dr. Cody. Although we clutch each other emotionally, we are separate, each struggling in our own private world of terror. I can't bear that it's true. I want my children. David does not want to lose me. I sense that he is torn apart himself but focuses on my pain and fear.

As I stand at the exit of the parking garage waiting for David to bring the car, I feel completely desolate. I watch the construction workers across the street and the people walking by. It's as if I am watching them from far off, as if we are not in the same universe. I feel angry that I have been robbed of ordinary life, of the world in which these people live. When David pulls up, I make myself move, get in the van, fasten my seat belt. I burst into tears but say nothing.

We return to our apartment to compose ourselves before getting the children. We call Alex and Sophie to tell them the news. They sound very upset but subdued, speechless yet speaking. Molly and Zach are fine, they say, and could spend another night with them. Instead, we ask if we can come for dinner. We need to see them and our children, to feel their love. We cannot be alone. And yet I am.

We must call my parents, too. I cannot bear to make this call. Two years ago they spent six months watching my sister Chris struggle on the brink of death, in and out of comas, her lungs filled with fluid, after the surgery to by-pass the blood clot near her liver. Somehow, she survived, but now I have cancer. I call them and begin to cry uncontrollably, as I have each time in my life that I have called them with bad news—Hodgkin's disease, the loss of hearing in one ear, my miscarriage. David takes the phone and, as always, explains the situation and begins his efforts to reassure them. How horrible that we have a routine for this. "The lump is small," he says, "and we caught it before it could even be felt." But I know they are stunned, sinking, not reassured. When I had Hodgkin's disease, they read in their outdated encyclopedia that there was no cure. David wants to fill them with encouraging information to ease their pain. I am told that when my mother heard my diagnosis of Hodgkin's disease she sat on her bed, silently folding clothes, with tears streaming down her face. I am torn apart by this image, which is now foremost in my mind. How can I do this to her again? I compose myself and tell them I'll know more on Tuesday. Would they please call my four sisters, as well as my brother in Texas?

We leave soon for Alex and Sophie's house in New Jersey. I cry as we talk about what to say to the kids. We agree to keep things simple until we can explain more clearly what is going to happen. I worry that I cannot hide my upset. David reassures me that they can manage seeing me cry. We arrive and there's lots of hugging. Because I know I could fall apart when Sophie hugs me, I say to her,

"Just don't ask me how I am." We laugh a little, and I am relieved that I have stayed composed thus far. We all sit in the living room and talk. Eventually I tell Molly and Zach that the doctor found a small lump in my breast that is cancer, that I will have to have surgery to have it removed, but that I will be fine. They say little. Mostly they ask for reassurance. Zach says, "You had cancer before and got better, right Mom?" "Right, honey." An hour later he says, "You'll be okay, right, Mom?" "Yes, Zach, I'm going to be fine. There's nothing to worry about." How can I keep saying this when I don't believe it for a minute?

The kids tell us about their day—working in the yard; reading to Grandpa, who cannot see well; making jewelry with Grandma. They leave to watch TV and we sit and talk with Alex and Sophie about what will happen next week. So often in the past twenty years, we've sat around their tiny kitchen table arguing politics, talking about the relatives, and luxuriating in our common pride in the children. That's what we do again tonight, and I feel comforted by the ritual of this meal and our talk, safe in the momentary illusion that life is normal. After we return home, Zach gets into bed and I sit and talk with him. He tells me that he's a little worried. He lets me rub his hair and reassure him. His trust breaks my heart.

April at our weekend house in the Hudson River Valley, two hours north of Manhattan, is wet and muddy.

The children take off quickly to be with their friends. Zach calls Jonathan, his best friend, a local boy who, in addition to being a good student, knows everything there is to know about trucks, tractors, and hard work. He's as much part of our family as Zach is of his. When we built our deck last summer, Zach and Jonathan helped with the construction, carrying boards and nailing them down. Molly and Stephanie, Jonathan's younger sister, quickly set up a refreshment stand, offering their very own fruit punch, carefully concocted in a large pitcher and then dripped in a trail through the kitchen and out the door. Afterward they hammered a few token nails themselves, at our encouragement.

Because the children are busy with their own activities most of the weekend, David and I are able to take long walks by ourselves. Everything around us is coming to life—crocuses will soon be followed by daffodils and forsythia. The buds are appearing on the trees, and the day lilies are beginning to poke up through the ground. I feel robbed of the ability to enjoy this experience. All my thoughts are focused on the fact that I have breast cancer; this fact is what I try to accept—not yet the surgery, radiation, or chemotherapy that lies ahead. I fear that I am dying, and all that is coming to life makes me sad. I will miss this spring. It's as if enjoying the present requires that I believe in a future.

David gives me space to express my fears, anger, and incredulity. He listens well to me now and says the kind of soothing things only someone with whom I've spent my adult life could say—that we've lived through this before and can do it again, that he knows how strong I am. When I had Hodgkin's disease, David was twenty-eight and we'd been dating for only a year. Although he was thinking of ending our relationship, he stayed with me, calmed me, even loved me. But sometimes he was silent when I needed reassurance, perhaps overwhelmed by the task of keeping his own feelings at bay, careful not to let himself know about his anger and his wish to flee. He simply read the *New York Times*—constantly, it seemed to me—while I repeated my fear that I would vomit. I felt terribly abandoned. Not now. He keeps his arm around me and accompanies me wherever my feelings insist I go—to the place of my darkest worries or of my deepest, now threatened, joys. This disease is not just mine; it sends its murderous threat into the entire body that is our family.

It is difficult to contemplate going to work on Monday. So much of my work concerns my relationship with my patients. I know how important it is that I be aware of what I am bringing to that relationship, and this week I will bring myself full of worry. It will be hard to sit in sessions with this information and act as if I'm fine; the prospect leads me to imagine a kind of war within me— competent therapist trying to subdue terrified baby. I decide against telling my patients about my breast cancer, except for the woman I met in the hospital, until after the surgery, when I am clearer about how my treatment will affect them. My real concern is that I may have to tell them news that will be frightening and disruptive to them. They don't need this cancer in their lives either.

David and I telephone new and old friends. I am not a person who copes in private. I need to talk, and I spare no one the details of my experience. Word spreads quickly over the weekend and I begin to get many calls. David and

Zina call from their vacation, managing as always to be available in a crisis. Jan calls from Florida, eager to lend her support in the way only someone who has had breast cancer really can. The friends who were at Harvard with us and helped me through Hodgkin's disease are particularly sobered; they share our outrage at the unfairness of my having to face cancer a second time. We call Craig and Nancy in Iowa. Both are doctors and, should anything adverse happen to them, we are the designated guardians of their two children. Craig was David's roommate in Cambridge when we were all graduate students. A loving friend who has kept in close touch through the years, he is incredibly smart and will help us make sense of the research on breast cancer. Because Nancy herself has survived ovarian cancer, she knows this treacherous territory and will be a great help.

My sisters and brother and my parents call. I cry with my mother in a way that I have not cried with her in years. I tell her how sorry I am to cause her more pain. She, as always, thinks not about her pain but mine. My father, because he cannot express his own feelings, tells me how upset my mother is. I say that I know how upset he is, too. I need this fact out in the open.

Neighbors drop by as well. Before David returns from the grocery store, John, our contractor, comes by to discuss repairs on our house. Within minutes I start telling him all the details of my diagnosis and my sister's illness. I realize that I'm out of control; here I am spilling my guts to someone I have not seen in a few years.

David returns and greets John warmly. We became friends the summer John and his crew built the addition on our house. John loved my plans for more bedrooms and worked from my drawings. Every morning we were awakened by the sound of John's trucks; we watched with fascination as the structure rose. John's father, newly retired from the construction company he started, presided over the table saw. Together they built the addition on this house, which has sheltered us through our happy times as a young family and our more recent sad times with my sister and her children. Now this house will shelter us during my breast cancer.

In the evening I lie on our bed upstairs, relaxed and aware of my body, aware that I like my body, especially my breasts. David and I have not been apart for a moment all day; we've talked nonstop, trying to adjust to the news of my cancer. We joke about my breasts, about how I don't really need them anymore, about what useless appendages they are, perhaps better gotten rid of for the sake of safety. I cry and David holds me. We sleep closer together than usual during the night. Although I love David's arms around me, I cry quietly when he touches my breast. I dream a lot, as if my psyche is busy integrating this terrifying news. When I wake in the morning, I enjoy for a few moments the light streaming through the windows. Then I remember that I have cancer, and I'm seized by such dread and fear that I cannot move from the bed. I finally force myself to rise, knowing that the kids need breakfast and normalcy. David makes cappucino and we sit and talk, feeling giddy again. Now it seems possible to envision the treatment as manageable, but I know this will change.

Just before my surgery for Hodgkin's disease, David and I spent five days on Cape Cod. David's advisor kindly lent us her house in Wellfleet as a retreat. At that time, I tried to gird myself for the abdominal surgery whose purpose was to remove my spleen, biopsy my lymph nodes, and determine the severity of my Hodgkin's disease. I remember my fear and my struggle to comprehend the idea of being cut open. And I remember my naive sense that this illness would somehow be romantic. Having read countless nineteenth-century novels as part of my doctoral program in English literature, I identified with the long-suffering female characters who died too young of consumption. I remember thinking, rather melodramatically, that if I had to die I had lived a good life and been loved by my family. I contemplated the painful possibility of never having children, but I prepared to face bravely whatever lay ahead of me. Of course, none of it worked out as I had imagined. I lived and gave birth to two children. But I was not heroic during my treatments and it was not romantic. It was a nightmare.

This time I recall a different character in those novels—the mother whose tragedy is not that she is dying so young but that she must leave behind her husband and small children. They stay by her side, a reminder of all she has to lose but a great comfort to her as she faces her death.

By the end of the weekend I come to a kind of clarity, not acceptance, really, but an acknowledgment of the fact that I have no choice—I either do this or risk dying. Having faced the necessity of surgery and treatment, I feel less conflict and now try to imagine how I will handle this surgery and the treatment. I vow not to be surprised this time when my noble determination gives way to self-pity and depression. I've been down this road before, and I know that things will soon become difficult in ways I cannot yet imagine.

We return to the city and I make a salad to take to Zach's basketball league dinner at a local school. We enter the building and I am overcome with a terrible sense of isolation. I can watch the children play basketball only because I am standing next to a friend who already knows about my diagnosis. When people talk to me, I respond mechanically. Eventually, I tell another mother about my breast cancer, and she doesn't seem to understand. I cannot bear how alienated I feel, and I decide to leave early with Molly. When David returns, he tells me that he was concerned about how quiet Zach seemed on the walk home. He asked Zach what he was thinking and Zach replied, "I wonder if I'll be able to make it into the National Basketball Association when I grow up."

Chapter two

Prospects

On Tuesday Dr. Cody reviews the pathology report with us. The tumor is small—1.2 centimeters. The margin of tissue on one side of the tumor was not "clean," suggesting to the pathologist that some cancerous tissue remained behind. Dr. Cody reads to us the characteristics of the cell, explaining that my cell type is not the best but not the worst—that is, neither the most aggressive type of cell nor the least. For some reason I choose not to inquire more about the characteristics of the cell, sensing, perhaps, that this piece of information is not all good news. He repeats that he would like to do a lumpectomy, a much less extensive surgery than a mastectomy, during which he would remove only a part of the breast tissue rather than all of it. He would want to follow a lumpectomy with radiation treatments of the area surrounding the site of the tumor if it's possible to do this radiation without overlapping the previously radiated area or, if it does overlap, without exceeding the maximum allowable dosage for a given area. He would guess that this is a stage-one breast cancer, but he can't be sure until he gets the information about the lymph nodes.

I ask if this breast cancer is a result of my previous radiation treatments. It's impossible to know, he replies. I explain that it seems related to me, that I received the most intense dosage of radiation right above the place in my breast where this lump appeared. I think I want the radiation to be the cause—it would explain why I have breast cancer when no one in my large, extended family does. Then again, when I posit radiation as the cause, I feel as if I'm carrying a time bomb, waiting for the next tumor to appear.

Dr. Cody suggests that I make an appointment with Dr. Chu, a radiologist at New York Hospital's Stich Radiation Center who recently presented a paper on treating former Hodgkin's disease patients with radiation a second time. He will obtain my radiation report from Peter Bent Brigham Hospital in Boston and have it sent to Dr. Chu before our meeting. Dr. Chu is a very aggressive radiologist, he says; if anyone can find a way to do the radiation, she will. If she argues against radiation treatments, we can be sure that they should not be done. Dr. Cody explains that the danger with too much radiation to an area is that the skin might ulcerate and not heal. It would be like having an open wound very susceptible to infection. Sometimes the radiation can be aimed in such a way that it will not affect previously treated areas. Taking a chance with radiation strikes me as unacceptable but not as unacceptable as my next thought: I may actually need a mastectomy. Although I have heard the possibility before, only now does it strike me as real. We set up an appointment for surgery on April 28—not yet clear whether Dr. Cody will do a lumpectomy or a mastectomy.

In the next week I speak to a friend, one of six women with whom I have met in a psychotherapy study group for the past ten years. She, too, has recently had a mammogram that indicated suspicious calcifications. I am stunned to learn of her situation but impressed by how thoroughly she is researching breast cancer in preparation for her biopsy. She tells me about *Dr. Susan Love's Breast Book;* the bible of women with breast cancer, it is filled with information and advice.

David stays up half the night reading this book. Our previous reading has convinced us that a lumpectomy with radiation, when appropriate, has the same rates of survival as a mastectomy. But we are bothered by the fact that, even in first-stage breast cancer, in which the tumor is less than two centimeters, the nodes are negative for cancer, and there is no obvious metastasis, there is only an 85 percent survival rate after five years. If localized treatments— either lumpectomy with radiation or a mastectomy— work, why aren't there better survival statistics? With the help of the references in Susan Love's book, David finds studies comparing the tissue samples of women whose cancer recurred with those of women whose cancer didn't.

Cancer returned in cases in which the margins surrounding the tissue that was removed were not clean, suggesting that some cancerous tissue remained in the breast. This is why surgeons now make sure that they leave a clean margin of tissue surrounding the site of the tumor, reducing the chances of a recurrence and probably resulting in a survival rate higher than the 85 percent reported on the basis of older data. Furthermore, he learns, many of the women included in the study that yielded these statistics were treated only with local treatments, not with chemotherapy. We plan to go over this with Dr. Cody.

My appointment with Dr. Chu is for Thursday, and David again arranges to come with me. I have assumed that it is normal for partners to accompany "patients" to these appointments, but I discover that many people come alone. Perhaps these women have no mates or their mates can't leave work. Perhaps they don't feel that they deserve support. Or perhaps they are braver than I.

To get to the Stich Radiation Center, we walk east on East Sixty-eighth Street past Sloan-Kettering, past New York Hospital and Rockefeller University, past Payne Whitney to what feels like the end of the earth or at least the end of hospital land. We enter a tastefully decorated foyer where the receptionist directs us to the basement. In the elevator there's a notice to patients: because the radiation machine is old and the new one has not yet arrived, appointments for radiation are being delayed. Oh great! You have cancer and need radiation but, because of technical problems, you will have to wait. Are they really putting off treatments designed to save people's lives?

When we reach the basement level, I speak to another receptionist who greets me as if she is expecting me. We sit in a huge waiting room where an overhead TV blares afternoon soap operas, a great diversion from our real-life dramas. I recall that at Peter Bent Brigham also the radiology department was located in the bowels of the hospital. It's like testing nuclear bombs in the desert   stay away from heavily populated areas. At the Brigham I waited for hours, surrounded by people of all ages crowded together, sick with radiation-induced nausea, and growing increasingly angry about the long wait. I remember the small children who had lost their hair, so unbowed and innocent as they were wheeled to their next treatment. The staff of the radiology department, except for the technicians who administered the treatments, was gruff and insensitive. I assume these people had not bargained on working with human beings, just x-rays. One doctor, upon hearing my reports of nausea and vomiting, told me that he had never had a patient as "bad" as I. Another routinely made me wait three hours, with his nurse making excuses for him. "He had an emergency," she said. But on every day that I have an appointment? I wondered. I tried to imagine a radiology emergency, with the doctor rushing to an accident, x-ray machine in hand. Another time I told the nurse how depressed I was feeling and asked to speak with a social worker. She panicked and called a psychiatrist, who met with me once and insisted that I did not need to talk to anyone, that of course I was upset. He offered to prescribe medication for depression.

This place seems completely different. The staff is pleasant. Today, at least, there are few patients, perhaps because of the shortage of machines. I am called by a nurse who gives me the uniform gown and slippers. She shows me to a room where I sit on a high examining table, feeling cold. David comes in and I talk with him from my great height. A doctor, a handsome, middle-aged Indian woman, comes in and takes my medical history. She is very formal and not friendly. Why is she keeping her distance? She examines me briefly and I joke nervously about the dots tattooed on my chest and my back from the previous radiation treatments. I explain my situation and the need to determine whether radiation is again possible. The two-page report that she received from the Brigham is not sufficient, she tells us. We will need to obtain the complete records, including all the x-rays, the design of the mantle that protected my heart and lungs, and the dosage and exact direction of the radiation. Eager to get on with this determination, I volunteer to contact my friend Martha, a doctor who lives in Boston, who should be able to expedite the sending of my records. By the end of the interview, I feel that my relentless friendliness and eagerness to be a helpful patient have persuaded this doctor to relax a bit with us.

She leaves the room, and David and I wait, talking about my options. I am here learning about the possibility of radiation for me, given the evidence that a lumpectomy with radiation provides results as good as those of a mastectomy, is less invasive, and certainly less disfiguring. But on the deepest level I still feel that more is better, that a mastectomy is better than a lumpectomy. It seems perfectly rational to get rid of the offending part. Isn't it better to throw out the whole apple if it's rotten? Why take a chance? Although I try to replace my hysterical reasoning with a more considered approach, my heart is not in it. The variety of options doesn't interest me, and I feel surprisingly indifferent to this one or that. I just want to get on with it.

The Indian doctor returns with Dr. Chu and a young Asian woman who is a resident. They each shake hands with us warmly and then get down to the business of examining me. I like the fact that all of them are women, and obviously competent women, engaged in this technical science. It's a funny scene. They begin a kind of hunting expedition of my torso, looking for the tattooed dots that are clues to where I was radiated. Although they are pleased about what they can piece together about my previous treatment, I begin to worry about how imprecise is the application of this science of radiology. I recall that my radiotherapists at the Brigham were corrected by their supervisor for directing the radiation too near my ear. A year later I was deaf in that ear. No wonder I worry about imprecision.

As I listen to Dr. Chu, I wonder if she is wearing a wig and not a very good wig at that, but she seems too engrossed in her work to care abut such vanities. Does she, too, have cancer? If so, how does she manage to work at such a high-powered job? My mind drifts to thoughts about my own patients and how I will juggle their visits if I go through radiation treatments. I'm struck by how much I love my work and how determined I am to continue to see patients. With Hodgkin's disease I had the opposite reaction. I was glad to take a break from writing a dissertation and from the endless doubts that plagued me about my choice of academics as a career. In retrospect, taking that break was a bad idea. I had too much time alone to think.

Dr. Chu continues to search my torso, talking to me about a woman in my situation whom they have just treated with radiation. They will need the more detailed records, but there might be a possibility of arranging a safe protocol of radiation treatments for this cancer. After a silence the resident asks, "How important is it to you that we save the breast?" Without hesitation I answer, "Not important. What's important is that I get well." What am I saying? That it's not important to me to save my breast? What universe am I in that I say this with assurance?

We leave and the resident's question echoes in my mind. I've given them the signal that I am not as intent on saving my breast as I know some women are. In fact, sometimes I seem determined to get rid of it. I sense that there's some uncertainty among these experts about using radiation and that I seem headed for a mastectomy.

On Friday we drive to the country and I am again in my own private world, working over all the ramifications of this breast cancer. During the ride I think about Molly and Zach and the future. Will I be around for them? Will I be at their graduations from high school or from college? Will I see them make choices about their careers and relationships? Will they marry? Will they have children? Will I still be alive then? I think about my parents and all they have suffered. If I die, they will lose a child, my children will lose a mother. I stop these thoughts because they are too dangerous; they will tear me apart.

I notice that I cycle through these thoughts as if they were ordinary, mundane. They occupy me the way other, ordinary thoughts used to—plans for dinner, the children's school work, my work, grocery shopping, calling friends. Soon all these ordinary activities will fall away, lose significance, not get addressed by me. Everything I love will be tainted by this illness. Even our house in the country, usually a haven from everyday pressures, will be no refuge. I long for the pleasure of musing about the future with confidence that it will come to be. But I'm on that desolate plain where nothing that is good or happy can be seen.

This weekend I try to adjust to the probability of a mastectomy. Friday evening, while David is visiting some friends, I climb into bed and read Susan Love's book. By the time David returns, I've read enough about treatments, survival rates, and recurrences to have worked myself into a full-blown state of panic. David, however, continues to read the book with a vengeance. Because its extensive information overwhelms and frightens me, he sifts through it and protects me from reading about all the more horrible things that could happen to me. Over the weekend new questions occur to me and I go to David, David to the book, and we learn.

It is remarkable how quickly I master this medical information when it concerns my life. I never considered myself good at science, but I see now that I merely lacked motivation. I have learned about staging and lymph node involvement. I have learned about precancerous conditions, which sometimes lead to cancer and can be discovered only if a woman has a biopsy. Knowledge of them gives a woman a warning to be watched closely; it also gives her something to worry about. I have learned that the pathologist determines how aggressive the cancer is by how differentiated the cells look (that is, how much they differ in appearance from normal cells), and by how many cells are dividing and how rapidly. The pathologist can also determine whether the cancer has invaded a blood or lymphatic vessel and whether there are dead cancer cells, both signs of a rapidly growing tumor.

David calls Craig for his opinion. Craig maintains that the choice between a lumpectomy with radiation and a mastectomy is essentially a choice between two very good options. Each treatment has excellent results with first-stage breast cancer. We are still working to understand the options even though we sense that my only option may be a mastectomy. We are also reading beyond the section on lumpectomies in Susan Love's book. I never thought we would have to read that far.

A mastectomy continues to seem completely barbaric to me. Although David still holds me at night, I lie curled up, as if holding myself together. In the morning I shower, put on my bra, and see my cleavage. I love my cleavage. My breasts are beautiful, a part of my body I have always liked. I feel incredibly sad. I imagine that in the future I will have to dress carefully to conceal myself. No more clothes that allow anyone a peek at my breasts. During the day David and I walk and talk. The children are about the house somewhere. We manage to feed them, see to their baths, and get them to bed. But it feels as if the two of us are alone, trying desperately to cope with the realities ahead of us.

回

We see Dr. Cody again on Tuesday. Having spoken to his colleagues, he is not optimistic about the possibility of repeating radiation with me. The danger of my skin ulcerating seems too great. He is now tending toward a mastectomy, as I am. We are still waiting for my records from Boston and for Dr. Chu's recommendation, but it is clear that we are reaching a consensus. Dr. Cody describes the mastectomy procedure and tells me what to expect. He will remove the breast and a number of lymph nodes under my arm, but he will not remove the muscle. The breast tissue and the nodes will then be examined at the lab to see if there is any further evidence of cancer. They will also do what is called an estrogen-receptor test, which will provide further information to help in the decision about whether chemo makes sense for me. Women with tumors that are estrogen receptive can benefit from taking tamoxifen, for example, which blocks estrogen and which researchers hope can stop the growth of malignant cells that are dependent on estrogen for growth.

Dr. Cody will have to cut some nerves in the course of the surgery, so I will probably lose sensation in part of my arm. Without lymph nodes to drain the arm, some women develop a condition called lymphedema in which the arm fills up with fluid. It will be important to avoid injury to that arm, such as cuts, bruises, or burns. I should not receive injections in that arm or even have my blood pressure taken there. After the surgery a temporary drain placed in the incision and connected to a small bag will collect the fluid, and the wound will be covered by a wide bandage. I will need to exercise regularly to get my arm back in shape.

If we decide on a mastectomy, I will need to consider whether I want breast reconstruction. Some women decide against it, but many feel it helps them adjust to the mastectomy. I can wait to decide, Dr. Cody explains, but, if the reconstruction is begun at the time of the mastectomy, only one further operation will be needed to complete the process. He suggests that I consult Dr. Michael Breckman, a plastic surgeon, to discuss the options. In any case, he has scheduled surgery for April 28, when Dr. Breckman can be present should I decide on reconstruction. Dr. Cody also gives me the names of several oncologists to discuss the question of chemotherapy.

Each step I take, each decision I make, moves me to a new plane where an entirely different set of questions awaits me. I'm to have a mastectomy. Will I have an implant? What does that mean? What will it be like? What doctor, what surgery, how many appointments? What pain, discomfort, or disfigurement? If I do not have reconstruction, there are other questions. What will it feel like to have one breast and a flat chest on the other side? What will I wear? What is a prosthesis? Where do you get them? As the day continues, my questions become clearer. I know that David rather than I will be on the phone to Dr. Cody in the morning. While I am reluctant to impose,

David feels entitled to attention. Instead I wait with my questions and suffer.

Dr. Cody is great. He gets on the line each time we call. He answers our questions and is patient while we learn, painstakingly, what he knows inside out. Now that a mastectomy seems likely, our questions are about why he and the books always mention chemotherapy along with a mastectomy. We have surmised that mastectomies are generally done on women with more advanced cancers than mine who obviously need chemotherapy. So why would I need it? What we discover is that the very nature of breast cancer is under discussion. Although localized treatments such as lumpectomy with radiation or mastectomy yield good survival rates, many researchers and doctors believe that breast cancer is not a localized disease but a systemic one—that is, a cancer that sends cells out into other parts of the body. It should therefore be treated with chemotherapy—with chemicals that reach all parts of the body, attack dividing cells such as cancer cells, and cause them to die. Dr. Cody confirms that there is growing sentiment that chemotherapy should be used in addition to a lumpectomy and radiation or a mastectomy, in many, though not all, first-stage breast cancers.

Although the statistics for first-stage breast cancer are reassuring, David finds them more consoling than I do; he is an optimist after all. Chemotherapy would boost my survival rate an additional three or four points. But I am skeptical. I remember saying when I had Hodgkin's disease that a 95 percent survival rate meant nothing to me. The cancer would either kill me or not, fifty-fifty. My current skepticism derives from the fact that, even though from 85 to 90 percent of my group will survive, and approximately 94 percent if chemotherapy is administered, who knows whether I will fall into that percentage?

Efforts to obtain my records from Boston become very complicated. Martha reports that the doctors in Boston would like me to be treated there. Although I may be a fine addition to their follow-up study, I'm furious at their arrogance. Don't they believe that first-stage breast cancer can be just as competently treated in New York, where I have a life? They send some reports but not the complete records. I do learn that they doubt this cancer was caused by my radiation treatments for Hodgkin's disease because the dosages I was given were fairly low. I'm not convinced though. Radiation is radiation, and I know that my skin, even today, feels as thin as tissue paper.

On Easter weekend in the country, I reflect on how my life circles back on itself. In 1976, my surgery was on Good Friday, and its scheduling lent itself to no end of Christian religious analogies—a last supper, stigmata wounds in my hands from the IVs, in my sides from surgery, and in my feet from incisions made during a diagnostic procedure. In the parable, there is a resurrection on Easter, so I obliged by coming around after my surgery. I remember a friend bringing me white Easter lilies. This Easter, the resurrection is harder to pull off. I must resurrect myself for Molly by putting aside my preoccupation and meeting her needs. No holiday escapes her, and I must meet the challenge of her expectations of a basket of candy, hidden in an unusual place, a festive breakfast table, and a cheerful mother. She will have her disappointments in the weeks ahead, but these I can prevent today. The effort to be alive for others seems herculean. Today I feel less afraid of death than of always feeling like this, detached and distant from my children. A living death.

We plan the day to Molly's satisfaction. She and Zach search for their baskets. Her breakfast plate holds a stuffed animal, a pink rabbit that she names "Flower," and Zach's holds a Queen Latifah CD. I love my children so much it hurts. In trying to act alive, I actually find my way to feeling again.

My friends get me through the weeks following the biopsy. My diagnosis has sent ripples throughout our world. After our immediate family and friends, there are our acquaintances—people from Molly and Zach's school, David's colleagues, and mine. Then there are friends of my family and friends of friends.

At first I feel only an outpouring of love and affection. Each day I return to a long tape of messages on my answering machine. David and I spend much of the evening talking to friends. I can see that I will need to set some limits on phone calls in order to preserve my time with the kids, but right now I need these conversations. Because my friends also are in shock, they can understand what a blow this is to me.

As time goes on, people's reactions become more complicated. Once they absorb the news, they begin to protect themselves from their own feelings of vulnerability. Sometimes this means convincing themselves that they are different from me. They reassure themselves that by eating carrots or exercising they will be spared. They ask questions that leave me feeling blamed. Is there breast cancer in my family? Do I eat red meat, or meat treated with antibiotics, or any meat at all? Does my diet contain fat? Do I exercise? Have I been under a lot of stress? I begin to feel set apart, isolated, and viewed as responsible for this cancer.

Of course, no one blames me directly. Nor do people sigh with relief if they decide that some aspect of my lifestyle must be the cause of my predicament. Most people would be horrified at the suggestion that they are blaming me. But I do feel judged and angry that people are considering their own psychic needs over my feelings.

Some people recount positive stories of survival. I hear about one woman who had breast cancer and bicycled twenty miles a day throughout chemotherapy; another who looked gorgeous the entire time; and a third who told no one of her diagnosis and acted as if her life were absolutely normal. Why are these stories not consoling to me? I have no desire to bicycle twenty miles a day. Nor do I expect to look gorgeous, let alone presentable. People want me to look and act as I always do, or better, so that they can ignore that cancer really hurts people, makes them look gaunt and unattractive, and sometimes kills them.

Others tell me stories of triumph over cancer that leave me with a whole new array of catastrophes that could befall me. One woman had breast cancer that was not treated with chemotherapy and the cancer spread to the other breast, but she is fine now. Another woman had a mastectomy twenty years ago and then a recurrence ten years ago, but she is fine. An eighty-year-old woman who had breast cancer once, skin cancer twice, and then uterine cancer also is fine. I am now filled with new worries about recurrences, aggressive tumors, skin cancer, uterine cancer, a future of new and untold cancers.

Still others don't seem to discriminate at all in the stories they relate; they tell me just any story that pops into their heads. Someone's uncle just died of lung cancer. Someone else's friend has leukemia. I'm treated to the details of someone's cousin's death and even an acquaintance's friend's mother's death. As I push down my panic, I try to remember that the person telling me is afraid. People dispel their anxiety by ridding themselves of these stories, giving them to me. Now I hold the fear they cannot bear to feel.

I suddenly realize that my children are going to have to deal with people's reactions as well. I tell Zach, very casually, that people are upset because I have breast cancer and they might say strange things to him. He asks what I mean, and I explain that people might speak to him in a very meaningful voice and say, "How *are* you, Zach?" He becomes very animated and his face lights up as he says, "Yeah, that already happened. When I went to Adam's house after school, his mother asked how I was and told me I should help myself to food in the refrigerator and that I was welcome in their house anytime. It was nice, but it felt a little weird."

It's a week since my consultation with Dr. Chu and my last meeting with Dr. Cody, and it is now time for my consultation with Dr. Breckman. The waiting room of his office is elegantly furnished, so different from the modern, sterile offices I have seen so much of lately. Of course, a plastic surgeon would have Oriental rugs and an ornately tiled bathroom. This is the medical specialty that makes the rich and famous "beautiful people." But the people waiting to see Dr. Breckman do not fit that bill. Some have obvious medical problems. One man's hands are wrapped in bandages, another walks with a limp. Some look worried; some not. It dawns on me that there is a difference between a cosmetic surgeon and a doctor of plastic and reconstruction surgery. I feel better knowing that Dr. Breckman does more than nose jobs and tummy tucks.

The office into which I am ushered looks a bit like a dentist's. It has a chair that reclines and cabinets full of silver instruments and medical supplies. One wall is completely mirrored. I'm about to hear about a whole new set of medical procedures of which I would happily prefer to remain ignorant. Dr. Breckman is middle-aged and a little soft in the body, not taut as one would expect of a plastic surgeon. He talks very fast. David has joined me and asks how he came to choose plastic surgery. Dr. Breckman explains that he studied another specialty but couldn't stand to see so many patients die. He prefers patients who live to appreciate his work. After some small talk, he sits on a stool and begins the speech he has surely given hundreds of times. He is not relating to me at all, not even relating to the prototypical woman with breast cancer. Otherwise he would assume that I am upset and address that fact. Instead, he gets down to technical business.

Although he prefers silicone implants, he no longer does them because of the controversy about their possible role in connective-tissue diseases. And because I might sue him, I suspect. There is also a reconstructive surgery in which a flap of tissue from your own body is used. I tell him that I have read about these surgeries and am not interested. Somehow, mutilating one part of my body to fix another doesn't make sense. He tells me that breast reconstruction with a saline implant requires two surgeries— one to insert a temporary implant, which can be done at the same time as the mastectomy, and another, later surgery to insert a permanent implant. The temporary implant has a valve into which he inserts a needle and injects saline (salt water) weekly. This procedure stretches the skin gradually and takes about twelve weeks. Temporary implants feel harder than real breasts. At the time of the second implant, many women have the other breast reduced. Without the reduction, the breasts will hang differently. It is also possible to have a nipple made from flesh taken from my thigh or some other part of my body. This procedure can be done in his office.

I can't comprehend half of what he is saying. I've never really tried to picture a mastectomy let alone a reconstructed breast. This implant idea strikes me as rather absurd, and the notion that women would have this done voluntarily simply to enlarge their breasts seems unimaginable. I express none of my feelings, and I go along with the idea that I will have an implant. I will. I will be cut up, sewn together, inflated. I can't bear to make yet another careful decision, so I'll just do this. I have read that in considering reconstruction I should ask the doctor to show me photos of his work. He does show me one photo of a woman standing naked from the waist up with two big breasts sticking straight out. She certainly doesn't look appealing, but then again who would, posing like that for a black-and-white snapshot?

I try to listen as Dr. Breckman talks about the different shapes of breasts there are to choose from, including one called a teardrop. Asian women tend to choose one shape and American women another. It is also possible to choose the size you want, within reason. He jokes that this is the time women can get the large breasts they've always wanted. I'm appalled. I can choose from a variety of breasts, and I have my choice of size and shape. I cannot believe that this doctor is talking to me like this. Here I sit, naked above the waist, in front of a mirrored wall, talking as if I'm choosing a dress. Doesn't this man know that I'm not here for fun? Doesn't he know that I'm about to have my breast cut off? Why isn't he mentioning what is really happening and how horrific this experience is for me? I'm a piece of meat. No, a mannequin. He is fiddling with my form. I'm not a person to him. He knows nothing about me. He wants to know nothing. I have a life. I have children. I went to Harvard just as he did. When we leave, David tells me that he liked Dr. Breckman. Sure, if you don't have cancer, I think, if you don't have feelings, if you're not living in a nightmare in which strange men are about to cut up your body.

Although the consultation has been incredibly upsetting, I spend little time thinking about reconstruction. I feel remiss for not weighing this decision carefully and talking to other women about their experience, but I lack the emotional energy. I'm dealing with the reality of cancer; whether I have one breast, a reconstructed breast, or a prosthesis inside my bra seems of little significance right now. Dr. Cody has said that most women seem to feel better with reconstruction. I make a decision based solely on the fact that with reconstruction I will be comfortable throwing on a T-shirt.

Because a month has passed since my biopsy, I need to repeat all the pre-op tests except the chest x-ray in preparation for the mastectomy. I also meet with an admitting nurse who talks to me about my upcoming hospital stay. She weighs me in at 113 pounds and determines that my height is five feet three inches. She writes down "mastectomy of the left breast." She is my age and talks with me about how many of her friends have had breast cancer. Because she seems attuned to the reality and impact of this disease, I let down my guard a bit. She carefully describes what to expect: the inpatient surgery unit; the gown, slippers, and robe; the surgery; the recovery room; the hospital stay. The more she talks to me, the more willpower I must exert to avoid falling apart. She has made all this too real, and I am hit with waves of fear and sadness. At the end of the interview she tells me that the nurse who works with mastectomy patients will be on vacation, so there will be no one making an effort to talk to me about the experience. I should ask a nurse to find one of the information packages they prepare for mastectomy patients. I receive this news as a declaration that no one will be there to take care of me and that I'd better be prepared to fight for myself. I leave the hospital feeling shakier than when I arrived, much like the feeling you have in realizing that you've just missed being hit by a car. How could such a straightforward conversation with an understanding nurse rattle me so deeply? It's not the prospect of my impending surgery but the thought of how alone I am in this that terrifies me. I can manage the surgery, but how will I manage the first day without my breast, the days of waiting to hear if they found cancer in my lymph nodes, the fear in the middle of the night that I will die and leave my children bereft?

During the week David and I speak to Zach and Molly about my upcoming surgery. We decide to keep the explanation simple and wait for their questions. I am not going to describe the mastectomy. The idea of having a breast removed seems like too much for them right now. It might be only for me that it's too much, but so be it. I will tell them more when it feels right to me. I explain that the doctor has to make a cut in my breast so that he can take out the small lump that is cancerous. He will then sew up the skin, and it will heal just like a cut. Molly grabs the shirt over her chest and scrunches the two sides together, as if joining the two parts of a torn shirt. "Like this?" she asks. "That's it," I say, noting to myself that she grabbed her shirt exactly where her breast is. Zach doesn't say much except to ask how long it will take until I'm better. I tell them I'll return from the hospital after a few days and stay home to recuperate for a week or so.

I visit a young friend and her new baby on Thursday. We talk about her labor and delivery and about my cancer. I hold the baby for a while. Then she nurses him. I am very moved by the experience. I cry but am surprised that these are not angry tears. They're more in gratitude for having had such a wonderful experience as a mother, though tinged with sadness that those days have passed. I feel what a grandmother must feel—proud of this young woman, reminiscent. I am going to lose a breast, but I've had this experience of my children sucking, feeling satisfied, and playing at my breast. I only hope I will get to be a grandmother.

We spend the weekend before my surgery in the country. Good friends are at their house nearby, but I don't want to see anyone. On Saturday morning David and I sit on our deck and watch the birds at the feeder. In the afternoon Molly and I drive to the nursery to buy some blue phlox and yellow violets for the bed in front of the house. In the afternoon I garden as if to prove something or perhaps to mourn something; as I dig in the earth, I imagine that I won't be able to shovel with my left arm in the future. Knowing that I tend to exaggerate, I push that thought aside and kneel down to join Molly as she digs small holes and excitedly plants the flowers we bought. Then I decide to take a bike ride. The last planting. The last bike ride. I'm quite melodramatic today. Zach has put new pedals on for me, and I manage to fall off as I try to negotiate them. What would Freud say? I have managed to get myself cut up and bruised three days before I'll be cut up and bruised in surgery. What I won't do to gain some control over what is happening to me, as if it's better to be the perpetrator of my own injuries than simply to submit to the upcoming surgery.

As I talk with David about the surgery, I weep with a deep sadness for my impending loss and I search for some resolve. How can I choose to do this? How can I consciously agree to have my breast removed? Everything in me fights this thought. I remember the surgical floor from last time. How will I go to the hospital in the morning, wait upstairs, walk through those doors and down that long surgical hall? How will I climb up on the table? And, like a lamb, bring myself to the slaughter?

This surgery will enable Dr. Cody to determine for sure the stage of my breast cancer. I think back to Hodgkin's disease and the more complicated staging process. First, I had a lymphangiogram, a procedure in which the doctor made an incision in each of my feet so that he could inject dye into my lymph system. He then took x-rays to get a complete picture of my lymph system so that he could look for tumors. The prospect of incisions in my feet seemed the most terrifying—no one had explained that my feet would be numbed first. When I had the abdominal surgery in which they removed my spleen and biopsied my nodes and organs, I was prey to endless bad jokes about my personality. I expect that the mastectomy will be less debilitating, but I feel myself preparing, as before, for the trauma that is surgery. I try various tricks—like imagining what Dr. Cody will do to me, as if envisioning his knife and the operation will make it less horrific. Then I tell myself not to think about it, that in a year I will have adjusted to it as I did with my earlier surgery. But then again, who misses a spleen when looking in the mirror?

I speak on the phone to my mother. She immediately understands my worries about what more they might find, and she tells me about her anxiety in the weeks before her hysterectomy a few years ago. I appreciate hearing this piece of her experience for the first time. I also speak to Gina in California. We have been close friends since high school. She wants to help, to be here. She would come. I just need to talk to her.

Saturday night David and I again lie on our bed in our room upstairs. I have not always appreciated how little he notices about my body, what I'm wearing, how my hair looks. But right now I love his indifference to the perfection or imperfection of my body. I actually believe that he does not care about this breast. He cares about what I must go through, but he does not mourn the loss for himself. Nor does he worry about feeling put off by my body, though I do know that somewhere he must have those feelings. After my radiation treatments in 1976, at dinner with a close friend, David described with great hilarity his trying to respond to my interest in sex when I had lost my hair and had a body covered with tattooed dots and magic marker lines. I wanted to feel normal, he understood. Although his story was painful to hear, I knew that he told it as a way to recover.

On Sunday I feel very agitated. I want to speak about underwear to women who have had a mastectomy. I can think only about bras and how I will dress until the implant is inflated to the size of a breast. I call a few friends who have had breast cancer, none of whom recall this problem. It's reassuring that they are busy in their lives and have no recollection of underwear concerns. But I feel alone, not believing I will ever be so busy as to forget this experience. I speak to one friend who recognizes that I am looking for more than underwear, that I am reacting to the nurse's warning that I will have little help adjusting to the mastectomy. She offers to contact SHARE and Cancer Care, organizations that provide support for cancer patients. I finally exhaust my desire to solve the bra problem and settle on one friend's solution—a bra with a pocket for padding on one side. I will also buy myself a silk chemise, something that will feel soft against my skin, look pretty, and cover me up. I laugh when I realize that I'm already planning my recovery and that I am staving off my terror about surgery by simply worrying about a bra.

We pack up to return to New York on Sunday afternoon. Zach and Jonathan play basketball until the moment we leave and Molly says goodbye to Stephanie and her friends. Gail and Bob, Jonathan and Stephanie's parents, come by to wish me well. It's awkward for all of us. We are close to them because we love each other's children. We offered our support to them when Stephanie had kidney problems at birth and Gail had cancer surgery. We have similar experiences and yet very different lives. Bob grew up on a farm, runs a landscape business, and works sixteen hour days. Gail grew up on Long Island and is the bridge between country and city, between Bob and us. I am touched by their effort to come and wish me well. Although I appear calm, I am screaming inside. As I embrace each of them, I wonder whether hugs will feel uncomfortable with one breast. Will I draw back as if to protect my breast or to keep people from feeling that part of my body?

I realize that I have resigned myself to this surgery. I have done my mental kicking and screaming, and it's time to quiet my angry resistance to the loss of my breast. There are certain things one simply must do, however grotesque and unimaginable, and this is one of them. Now there is only the event to focus on—the surgery. Everything drops away but the steps I must accomplish to get myself there—see my patients, pack my suitcase, make lists of phone numbers and the kids' schedules and activities. The single-mindedness of what I must do somehow calms me.

Chapter three

LOSS

I see patients on Monday and Tuesday before surgery on Wednesday. My friends find me overly conscientious about work and have suggested that I take time off to prepare for surgery, but I know that work will distract me. Before Molly was born on a Tuesday at 5:00 AM, I worked Monday evening until 9:00 PM. I joked that I could have been back at work on Tuesday. It helps me right now to have work to focus on. Although my mind seems to wander to my surgery at the beginning of sessions, I am usually able to make myself concentrate enough to become involved in what my patients are saying. They know that I am having some kind of surgery and will be out for ten days, but I choose not to tell them about my breast cancer until I will be here with them to talk about their reactions and until I have a sense of how my treatment might affect my work. I listen to what they imagine—everything from bunions to breast cancer. My impending absence is worrisome to them and we concentrate on their fears.

David and I spend Monday and Tuesday evenings solidifying our arrangements for the kids. Jerry will come over at six o'clock on Wednesday morning to get them to school. He is Zach and Molly's uncle, having been married to David's sister for many years, though now divorced. Their friends' parents will drive them to school and our babysitter, Eve, will meet them after school. Our neighbors Paul and Arnhild will give them dinner and spend the evening with them until David returns from the hospital to put them to bed. I hope to be home on Friday.

On Tuesday I am oddly excited, as if I am preparing for a vacation. I look forward to this time at home in spring, to walks in the park, until it dawns on me that I will not be on vacation but will be recovering from surgery. This is not excitement; it's mild hysteria.

Phone calls keep coming in and I feel again how loved and supported I am. I put on the answering machine at eight o'clock so that I can say goodnight to Molly and Zach and then go to bed early. I'm never good at separation, always finding in goodbyes more finality than is indicated. I brace myself for talking with each of them. I hug Molly and feel her body against mine. Will she notice the difference after the mastectomy? I hope nothing ever happens to her body. Will I see her develop into a woman and be able to admire her beautiful breasts without fear for her?

Molly seems more focused on the separation from me than on the surgery. Since I broached the subject last week, I have heard nothing from her or Zach about the fact that I have a tumor in my breast. Have they put it out of their minds or composed some primitive but manageable picture of it for themselves? Zach says that he has no questions and insists that the impending separation doesn't bother him: "It's just two days, Mom. No sweat." I tell him that, even so, I will miss him. I hold back the urge to hug him desperately. I go into my room and sob uncontrollably. I pack a nightgown and robe, a toothbrush, books, phone numbers, and a photograph of Molly and Zach. David comes to say goodnight and I ask him if he remembers the day of Molly's birth when Zach refused to go to school, distraught because he believed Molly and I were going to live in the hospital forever. After all, we had told him that I was going to the hospital but not that I would return. Maybe now I'm the one who's worried that I won't return.

It is a night of nightmares. David hears me moaning in my sleep and holds me. I dream that after surgery Dr. Cody informs me that he had to sew my arm permanently raised over my head. He is very sorry. In another dream I witness a woman being stabbed by a man. She lies on the ground dying as blood streams out of her wound. It seems that my dreams have lost all subtlety. No longer is their meaning hidden from me until I untangle my associations. Now their plots have been reduced to battles between good guys and bad guys, with one difference: the good guys in the dreams, the doctors, are the ones who are hurting me.

The alarm wakes me at five o'clock, and I go through the motions of brushing my teeth and dressing. My body feels numb. I must exert myself to get my limbs to move— I feel tired, spent, similar to how I feel when I've worked too hard the previous day or cried myself to sleep. I repeat over and over to myself that I cannot do this, but I sense how feeble my resistance has become. Jerry arrives. He is so kind to me. I know that he sees my fear but there's nothing to say. The kids rise groggy eyed, and Zach gives me a perfunctory hug, Molly a long and clinging one. Jerry takes over and David and I leave, acting as if this is some routine expedition.

We enter the hospital through the main entrance and are directed to the admitting room. We wait with eight or so other people, including a girl of about ten years. Eventually I am summoned to a small room where I answer the usual questions and then am asked if I have a living will. I say, matter-of-factly, "No, but that would probably be a good idea." This seems a rather tactless moment to raise the subject. I picture myself hooked up to a machine, a living death, because I had no living will. Perhaps they could move this part of the routine to the pre-operation stage. She will send us the information.

We take the elevator to the presurgery waiting room where the nurses seem busy but friendly. What a great

change. They seem like housewives preparing for the day.
I'm given a shopping bag for my belongings, shown to a
dressing room, and given the uniform. Prison again. After
I've dressed, I rejoin David in the waiting room. It's like an
adult pajama party here, a ludicrous gathering of men in
green and women in blue-striped seersucker robes. I do
like the robes. I would wear one in real life.

We sit in oversized leather chairs. The TV blares over
our heads, but no one watches it. I am called by a nurse
who takes me to a small office where she records my medical history. She tries to put me at ease by talking about this
surgery as routine and simple. She sends me back to the
waiting room and tells me it will be a few hours. I feel
angry that I have been made to come here so early to sit in
this cold room waiting. I busy myself watching people and
wondering about their stories. Illness is the great leveler.
Here sit men and women, young and old, rich and poor.
One woman sits alone reading the *New York Times*.
Another older woman talks animatedly with her husband.
The girl we saw downstairs sits with her young mother
and her grandmother, who is not much older than I. The
grandmother seems to be the one who attends to her. The
girl appears to be only too familiar with this hospital; she's
obviously been here before.

Dr. Cody comes earlier than expected, dressed in his
surgical gown and hat. He seems to be on quite friendly
terms with the staff and asks a nurse to find us a room in
which we can talk. He reassures me again that I will be
fine, repeats the facts about my tumor, and goes over the
statistics again. He does not expect to find anything
unusual. David joins the discussion, consoled as always by

information. I just sit, trying to calm my terror and discover the proper etiquette for this moment. This man is about to remove my breast. Losing my mind would seem like proper etiquette. I hear Dr. Cody discussing clean margins. He mentions again that he will have to cut some nerves in my arm, so I may have an area that is permanently without feeling. Sometimes I wish I could be permanently without feeling. I express my worry about the other breast, not saying what I really think, that he should just remove my other breast now and be done with it. Although my chances of getting breast cancer in the other breast are slightly increased, he reminds me, they are still small, and there's no indication of a problem there right now. He will biopsy that breast in the course of the surgery. He shakes our hands and tells me that he will see me in the operating room.

David and I return to wait. The nurse comes shortly to tell me it's time, and David accompanies me to the elevator. He hugs me goodbye. I cannot bear the moment of our parting. I feel completely alone in the elevator, though I am surrounded by doctors and nurses. I get off on the surgical floor that takes me to the doors I must pass through to walk down the hall to the operating room where I must get up on the table. It's not just prison, it's death row. How do condemned inmates willingly walk to their execution? This is not an execution, I tell myself. Still, I cannot bear the thought of what is about to happen to me.

I do it. I walk through the big swinging doors and down the hall filled with doctors and nurses in green surgical clothing. Once again I am saved by the mundane. The anesthesiology resident introduces himself, asks me a list of questions, and tells me that I can't possibly be allergic to cortisone. At least some things are familiar. I explain that, after taking cortisone for hives, my rash got worse. Yes, it might not have been the cortisone, who knows? The surgical nurse tends to me and I realize that I need this person, the only woman here, to stay close. I sit on the cold table in my surgical hat, looking absurd, noticing how many young male doctors are here. When I had surgery for Hodgkin's disease one of the interns told me later that the doctors were reluctant to cut into such a nice, young body. Certainly that will not be how they think of my body today, marred as it is by the scars of surgery and childbirth. It will be easier for them to objectify me now that I am a woman of a certain age. I think of those seventy-year-old women with breast cancer who are told that it won't matter if they lose their breasts. As if there is anyone for whom losing a body part doesn't matter.

Dr. Cody arrives and greets me. He talks with the residents, who clearly like him. For them this is just another day at work. I am ready now; there's no turning back on this decision. Dr. Cody comes and stands by my side. I tell him that I dreamt about him—nothing good, I say. He understands how I feel, he says; all patients about to undergo surgery fear they are going to die, but I will be fine. It had not consciously occurred to me that I might die, but it makes sense that I could feel that way. And I did have fantasies of being executed. Isn't that a fear of death? I appreciate Dr. Cody's attempt to comfort me, and I trust him. The anesthesiologist introduces himself and fiddles with my arm as he tries to find a vein for the IV. He finally begins the anaesthesia. I feel woozy and the room begins to spin. Although I am soon out, I am in a dream that makes me feel as if I'm awake, a pleasant dream in which I feel warm and seem to be floating in space.

I begin to regain consciousness in the recovery room. I feel only excruciating pain, radiating from my left side. I cannot get comfortable. I sense the approach of a nurse coming to give me medication. I drift in and out of sleep. The pain is relentless, pounding, everywhere. I am saved over and over by sleep. The line between waking and sleep fades, and I move fluidly from intense pain to oblivion. Eventually I hear the nurse say that they are going to take me to my room. They slip some contraption around my body, which makes me feel as though I am in traction, and succeed in transferring me from bed to cart. I sleep through the journey and then again feel myself being lifted and transferred to a bed. I am in my room.

I sleep most of the day. David is with me, but I am in my own world, my own pain. Nurses come and go to check my blood pressure, take my temperature, and empty the bag that collects the fluids from the drain placed in the wound. I am near the door in a space barely large enough for a bed, let alone a chair. They obviously crammed an extra bed in here, and I am in it. I sleep on and off. A nurse coaxes me to go to the bathroom, as have the nurses all evening, but I am not ready. David goes home at some point. My head is still swimming; the pain is everywhere. I am not coherent enough to sort out clearly what is around me. I hear noise from the hall. I feel as though I'm in the middle of a huge kitchen where workers are clattering stainless steel pots together. The room is brightly lit, and women in other beds talk to each other and to the nurses. I try to turn on my side, but the pain is excruciating. I prop some pillows under my left arm and try to sleep again.

The pain increases and I ring the bell for a nurse. Nothing. I wait. I ring again. When a nurse finally comes, I request pain medication. She promises to bring some but does not return. No one comes. I ring and wait, again and again. Finally a nurse brings me some Demerol, and I sleep for a while. I wake because I need to go to the bathroom, and I call the nurse to help me out of bed. No one comes. I feel helpless and angry, but mostly helpless. Finally, a male nurse's aide peers through the curtain at me, looking annoyed. I explain that I need help getting to the bathroom, and he tells me that they are very busy. I will have to go by myself. If I fall, I should call them.

I wait for a while, holding back tears of rage. Finally, I decide to go by myself. I sit up gingerly on the side of the bed. Everything hurts. I feel as if I'm going to faint. When the dizziness passes, I stand shakily. It takes me some time to arrange the pole with the IV. I still feel faint, but I move slowly to the hall and walk very carefully, grateful for a railing along the wall. The aide sees me, and I imagine that he feels some guilt as he looks at me. At least I hope he does. I make it to the bathroom and lower myself onto the toilet seat where I sit for a while, trying to get my body to work. I finish and begin the journey back to my room, frightened because I still fear that I will fall. I make my way back and carefully lift myself into bed, untangling the

IV and settling myself down. I am still enraged, but eventually I drift back to sleep.

When I wake, I ring for the nurse to request medication again. No answer. I ring again and wait. The incessant clatter continues, and the bright lights remain on. Why won't they make it quiet and dark so that people can really sleep? The pain is building and I cannot get help. I begin to cry. A nurse finally comes and I try to compose myself. She sees that I am distraught, says nothing, but looks upset. She is helpless, too, I imagine, helpless with overwork and unable to do more than the most minimal nursing. Now, on top of her work, she is confronted with evidence of having upset me. She brings my medication and leaves.

At 6:00 AM the nurses wake me to take my blood pressure, my temperature, and my pulse. I wait for David but know that visiting hours do not begin until 11:00 AM. The time seems interminable. My already fitful sleep is interrupted with ever increasing frequency. One shift finishes its tasks so that the next can begin. Not a single nurse ever attempts to talk to me. I feel tired, angry, almost frantic. It would be difficult to design a scenario more likely to make a vulnerable person feel out of control. I really need help and can get no response. I am as much an object to the staff as is my pitcher of water or my adjustable bed; and, even when they respond to my call, I am just another task, not a person in pain.

Dr. Cody comes by early. I tell him that the night was horrendous, but I conceal how distraught I really feel. He looks over my chart, drains the bag of fluid, and says he is pleased with the healing. He urges me to walk about as much as possible and reminds me to do the exercises to strengthen my arm—walking my fingers up the wall and pushing to reach farther each time. I repeat my wish to go home the next day and, glancing about the room, he agrees. The nurse will teach me how to drain the bag and measure the amount of fluid in it; I should keep track of the amount. Dr. Breckman also stops by to check my wound.

David arrives at eleven o'clock to spend the day. He's fresh from home and the children. Although I'm relieved to see him, I envy his pleasant morning, so different from the past five hours I've spent here. He finds me in tears. I complain that I've never spent a worse night, that I feel assaulted, neglected, and trapped in this small space. David can't believe they've put four people in this room. In the next bed is a woman of my age who looks like she's dying. Her hair is thin, and she's so weak that she cannot walk. From what I hear her doctors say, I gather that she has an advanced cancer. Across the room are two more beds. In one is a woman of about sixty who is now up and walking about. Next to her is a woman of seventy whose leg is bandaged. She has a private-duty nurse who sits by her bed all day. I have no interest in getting to know any of these women. All I want is to be home in my own bed. I ask about Molly and Zach, who, David tells me, went off easily to school this morning. Molly had trouble settling down for bed last night, so he read to her for a long time, and he let Zach stay up and watch TV with him. I tell him that I'm worried about seeing them when I'm in such bad shape emotionally and that I hope I'll feel better in a day.

By afternoon I do feel better, and I learn that the sixty-year-old woman across the room has just finished chemotherapy and is recovering from surgery and doing well.

She's worked hard at getting herself moving and walks up and down the hall often. The woman with her leg bandaged is worried about whether her skin graft will heal but complains little and mostly fills us in on the articles in today's newspaper. Her daytime private nurse loves to talk and tries to engage me in conversation. Although I feel closed off, I try to relax and appreciate their kind inquiries and interest in the photograph of Zach and Molly on my bedstand. After all, haven't I been complaining that no one will talk to me?

Flowers keep arriving all day. People call to see how I am doing or to ask where to have flowers delivered. I feel less stripped of my self, less alone when I imagine the people in my life outside this room—my children at school, my friends at work, my family. Betsy, who has been my friend since graduate school, visits and brings flowers. She is refreshingly practical. In Cambridge, after my surgery, she helped me wash my hair in the sink in my room.

I know this visit is hard for Betsy. She nursed her mother through a horrific brain disease that eventually killed her, and she cared for two elderly aunts until they died. We walk to the sunroom and sit and talk. It feels good to be up and about, but I soon tire and return to bed, leaving David talking to Betsy about history and knowing that Betsy, however busy, will oblige him.

Jan arrives before dinner. I remember how stunned I was when I learned of her breast cancer diagnosis three years ago. At the time I thought it was a death sentence. It never occurred to me that I too was a candidate for breast cancer; somehow, despite my own history of cancer, I managed to keep this possibility from entering my mind.

Jan's consistent good nature is something I will never duplicate, but I am glad to have a friend who has traveled this path to mastectomy and beyond, and has done so with such equanimity. Jan suggests we order food from a restaurant rather than leave me to a hospital dinner. While David is getting the food, we talk. Jan lets me touch the breast where she has her implant, and I'm relieved that it feels to me like a real breast. She demonstrates that she has completely normal movement in her arm. Most reassuring, though, is her presence. She looks great. She is animated and full of stories about her students and her academic work. We talk a lot about our children and their reactions to our breast cancers. Nothing could be more calming than her visit.

David returns with a Mediterranean feast—pita bread, babaganoush, tabouli, and olives. While we enjoy our meal together, our friends Pam and Roger surprise us with a visit. They bring flowers and I am very touched that they have come. Thursday is the night we often have had dinner with them. Roger is a psychiatrist who, in his personal life, censors few of his thoughts. He jokes about breasts and I find his outrageousness a relief. One of his friends recently had a mastectomy. When I ask how she managed, he answers without hesitation, "She became psychotic."

While they are with me, one of Dr. Breckman's residents comes by and seems skeptical of my intention to go home the next day. I react like a caged animal at the thought of another day here. Everyone leaves but David, and I ask him repeatedly, even after he has already agreed to do so, to call Dr. Breckman and Dr. Cody to make sure that I can go home. I want to throw things, but I'm in a room with four people. So I throw my words at David, trying in vain to get him to help me out of this, not just this room, but this whole experience. I turn my request that he call into an attack on him, as if he is at fault. He becomes quiet and withdraws, a signal to me that I've gone too far, that I have pushed him away and am now alone. I recall that at Peter Bent Brigham, after holding myself together through the Hodgkin's disease diagnosis, I broke down when I laid eyes on my dismal hospital room. Such small details—a depressing room, another day in the hospital— become the locus of my need for some control over my surroundings, over what is happening, over something. Without such control, I feel dehumanized, defenseless, the way I imagine people in such encounter groups as EST feel when they are not allowed to leave the room to go to the bathroom, as if being reduced to a state of helplessness and vulnerability will somehow be good for them.

Luckily, David understands my frustration. He recalls how fifteen years ago, after his knee surgery and a few days in the hospital, he phoned me at midnight in tears, feeling vulnerable and abandoned. Why do two days in the hospital leave a person so raw? Is it the physical assault of the surgery, the unnerving reminder of one's mortality, the impersonal care, the separation from reassuring routines of daily life?

After David leaves to make the calls and tuck the kids in bed, I overhear the woman with the skin graft talking to the nurse about her husband, who is living in a nursing home. He called earlier and she told him that she couldn't talk because the nurse was changing her dressing. Now she worries that she hurt his feelings. She calls him back and talks lovingly to him, inquiring about his activities and his health. Were I given to inspiration, this woman would be it. She has endless medical problems, yet she avoids self-pity and manages to be loving. I feel like a spoiled baby compared with her.

This second night is better. I can get to the bathroom alone; I am in less pain; and I know to call for medication the moment I sense the last dosage wearing off. But the second morning is more aggravating. I hate the early morning routine. I am awakened repeatedly by nurses and aides who check my temperature and blood pressure to be sure that I'm all right, though it would be hard to know that they cared. Another of Dr. Breckman's residents appears and insists that I cannot go home. I wait for either Dr. Breckman or Dr. Cody to come by and sign my release, like prison again. I wait through breakfast, a morning sponge bath, journeys down the hall, and a few phone calls. Finally, Dr. Breckman comes by, having received a message from Dr. Cody approving my release. It's obvious that my leaving so soon makes no sense to him, but he defers. He checks my wound and tells me that it is healing nicely. I don't look. I am aware of the drain and the bandages, but it is as if they do not connect to my lost breast. I am focusing on recovering from surgery right now, and I give little thought to the nature of that surgery. I'll deal with my lost breast later.

I need the nurses to go over the instructions on how to empty the bag of fluid and measure the amount, but they are too busy. David arrives and urges me to hurry because Jerry is waiting in the van and can't stay parked long. David is operating on "real world time." He actually thinks that events will happen when he needs them to or when we've been told they would.

I sit dressed in stretch pants and a shirt. A friend told me to bring a shirt with buttons down the front because I would be unable to lift my arm to put clothing over my head. I've pinned to the waist of my pants the rubber bag that collects the fluid from the wound and tucked the thin plastic tubes under my shirt. I comb my hair and apply a little blush to my cheeks, but I see that I still look very pale and worn out. I'm going home and, aside from my surgeons, no one on the hospital staff has spoken to me about the mastectomy, the postoperative adjustment, or what to expect with the healing. No one has even asked me how I am doing. How little it would take to make me feel better. I still remember a brief exchange with a resident in Boston during my treatments; undaunted by the worry in my twenty-six-year-old face, he reassured me that I would be all right.

My roommates wish me well. They have been very kind to me, the youngest. In asking about my children, they perhaps sensed that this topic would be like a lifeboat in the dark ocean of my worry. They are happy to see me improving and assure me that I will be fine, even while knowing that they themselves may not be.

David and Jerry help me to the van, and I realize that I am not doing as well as I had thought. The hospital corridor, with all its clatter, was quiet compared with the street, where I cannot screen out the blare of traffic and sirens, all sounds coming at me with equal intensity, with none receding to the background. My steps are tentative, my body weak and unprotected, as if my skin has been stripped away and I am all exposed nerve endings. I feel slightly embarrassed with Jerry. It's not my mastectomy. It's my rawness. I feel so exposed, like the people in war photographs whose faces give you a glimpse of their private terror.

I am so relieved to arrive home. Our bedroom, which overlooks Riverside Park and the Hudson River beyond, is clean and bright. David and I brought all my flowers home in a bucket of water, and I arrange them in vases. I get undressed, avoid looking at my bandaged chest, and put on my own nightgown. I climb into bed and plan to sleep until Molly and Zach arrive home from school at half past three. I feel peaceful. Right now there are no decisions or obligations except to heal. I sleep solidly and then awaken, knowing again that I have been busy dealing with this trauma in my dreams.

Molly and Zach arrive home, and we have a happy reunion. Zach seems a little shy, perhaps sensing my fragility. Molly is bursting with things to tell me. They sit on my bed and visit for a while, and then they are off to their own affairs. Later, they bring me dinner and say goodnight so that I can sleep. It feels strange not to cook and spend the evening with them. But even this sense of loss is fleeting. My energy is too tied up with taking care of myself.

On Saturday I sleep most of the day. The phone rings and the doorbell announces the arrival of flowers and gifts.

I feel quite loved, surprised by all the attention and amused by the ingenuity of my friends' gifts: a package of hip magazines including *Billboard*, *Spy*, and *Z*; a set of *I Love Lucy* videos to make me laugh à la Norman Cousins; a plastic pet tornado labeled "Fenced Fury" (you shake the capped container until the "snow" inside begins to swirl into a funnel), the perfect gift.

David spends time with the kids in the morning, and they have plans with other people in the afternoon. His parents come for a visit and I feel happy to see them, though my stamina is limited. I think about how my cancer leads others to recall their own earlier experience. Alex lost his first wife to rheumatic heart disease when David was four and Adrienne was eight. He cannot bear to see me sick. He feels for David because he has been in this place as the husband. And he wants to protect Zach and Molly from the loss he saw his own children suffer.

Sophie sits by my bed and we talk. I love her dearly, but today I am aware of other, complicated emotions as well. I feel envious of the good health she enjoys at the age of seventy-five. I have cancer for the second time and I'm only forty-four. I am so much more experienced at serious illness. Right now she sees in the future a far brighter landscape than I. We talk about underwear. She generously offers to shop for the silk chemise that I imagine will make me feel better. I can't seem to talk or listen very well today. We eat the dinner that Alex has prepared, and they leave discussing the size of container in which to bring us weekly family-sized portions of spaghetti sauce.

On Sunday morning an old friend, Marilyn, visits me in my bedroom as she did when each of the children was born. Our neighbors drop in, and the phone rings all day. Later, Martha visits from Boston. I thank her for the effort she made to gather my records, and we talk about how I made the decision to have a mastectomy without ever learning of Dr. Chu's recommendations upon seeing my records. The children join us on the bed for the picnic of bread, cheese, fruit, and dessert that Martha brought. It helps that she is a doctor, but today I need her as a friend.

After Martha leaves, Molly comes in, agitated. I ask what is wrong, and she angrily tells me that it isn't fair that I'm getting all the presents and attention and she's getting none. Her voice is shrill and loud and her anger escalates quickly. I feel attacked by her and snap at her, telling her that I just had surgery, as if that means anything to her. Then I begin to cry, overwhelmed by the intensity of our interaction. She looks devastated, and I know immediately that she feels she has hurt me. I take her in my arms, and we both cry and hug each other. I tell her that it's okay, that I'm glad she told me that she feels angry. I tell her that I understand that it's very hard right now and that she does need more attention from me. We spend some time together, and I interest her in doing certain jobs such as bringing me juice and making sure that I do my arm exercises. I have her back, and I am grateful that she made contact with me through her anger, sorry that I folded on her and left her feeling so destructive.

On Sunday afternoon David and I take a walk in Riverside Park. It is only four days since my surgery, but I am eager to walk outside. As we leave our building, we meet several people we know, some who have heard about my breast cancer, some not. From their reactions, I know that I look frail. As we walk in the park, David and I recall my first walk after my laparoscopy in Boston. I was transferred from the hospital in Boston to the clinic at Harvard, and ten days passed before I could go out. I then embarked on a harrowing walk that lasted the distance of only a block. Here again is that feeling so familiar after surgery: the world seems unreal, filled with so many strong and active people beside whom I feel weak and vulnerable. Today I am afraid of all the activity, of people jogging and walking fast, rushing by on bikes and in-line skates. I move very slowly, leaning on David's arm, and we make it to the garden at Ninety-first Street. There we rest and try to enjoy the early spring flowers, but I soon tire and need to begin the journey back home. It is as if we are in the country walking, so separate are we from everyone else.

On Monday I have an appointment with Dr. Cody. I meet David at Dr. Cody's office, and he tells me that he left a message for Dr. Cody earlier. I know he couldn't bear to wait all day for the pathology report, but he failed to obtain an early bulletin. We are focused primarily on whether any of my lymph nodes tested positive for cancer. I am very anxious, holding myself still again. David reassures me, and himself, that, even if nodes are affected, the cancer is still treatable. My mind wanders to the thought that Dr. Cody has now seen and touched the inside of my body. Just like the dentist, I tell myself, only farther into my body than my mouth.

When Dr. Cody arrives, he seems particularly relaxed. The nodes are negative, he tells us. It's a moment of wonderful relief, which he shares with us. He takes off the bandages around my chest, and I steel myself to look at my breasts. He removes the drain, asking about the amount of fluid I collected each day from the wound. He then removes my stitches. I am acting as if I am fine. I feel him cut the stitches. I look at my breast. There is a neat scar across the center of my left breast area and because the implant has already been inflated slightly, there is a very small mound on my chest. It is still my body. I am basically intact. And this is not as gruesome as I had feared. Dr. Cody is pleased with how well I am healing and tells me that I can get dressed and then we'll talk.

In his office Dr. Cody reviews the pathology report with us. Some cancerous tissue had remained in the breast after the biopsy. Because the total size of the tumor is calculated by adding this additional tissue length of 0.5 centimeters to the length of the tumor and not to the width, the tumor is considered to be 1.7 centimeters. Having seen the tumor during surgery, he thinks that in reality it is more like 1.5, which he still considers small. He again describes the cell type as not the best and not the worst. I silently focus on "not the best" and begin to feel frightened all over again. He reminds us that you can have positive nodes and never have a recurrence or negative nodes and have one. Sometimes he ruins my fun, I think. David presses for more reassurance, and Dr. Cody admits that it is certainly better that I have negative nodes.

He begins to talk about our treatment options. I tell him that I have an appointment on Friday to see Dr. Anne

Moore, one of the oncologists he had recommended. He assures me that I will like her, and he will be interested in her opinion about chemotherapy. He feels that in my situation we could go either way. Because the tumor is small and I have had a mastectomy, any stray cancer cells could probably be handled by my immune system. Chemotherapy produces the most marked improvement in women with more advanced cancers, and the statistical increase in survival rates for women in my situation is only three to four percentage points. Still, it is an increase. And chemo is generally more effective in premenopausal women, so it is worth considering. Often, healthy, young women handle the chemo well and continue their lives with little interruption. He suggests we meet again after I see Dr. Moore.

We leave his office and, as always, I cry. What is it about seeing him that leaves me so upset? David does not have this reaction. It's those statistics. An 85 percent survival rate in the first five years still doesn't sit well. Perhaps I'm being greedy, but I want at least the 95 percent I had with Hodgkin's disease. Breast cancer seems more insidious, more likely to return. Yet chemotherapy has always been my most dreaded fear.

I cannot bear another decision, and now there's another decision to make. David tries to tell me that I just received great news—negative nodes. Although I resist enjoying this relief, I do hear him. The part of me that is able to hope, even a little, clutches this strange possibility that I might come out of this and be all right.

David and I actually have a good day together walking about the city. After seeing a movie intended to distract me, we happen past a wig shop. The wigs don't look as bad as I had expected. I go in and quickly try on a few before fleeing the shop. I'm just getting my feet wet. David goes off to meet the kids, and I walk to Bloomingdale's to find a soft, athletic bra with no underwire. The experience in the dressing room is painful. I keep worrying that someone will come in. It's as if I'm doing something wrong and I don't want to be caught. Do I actually feel guilty about losing my breast? Or is it shame? I try on bras while attempting to ignore the sorrow I feel when I look in the mirror at my slightly convex, black and blue chest with a scar across the middle. I manage to buy only one bra, realize how completely exhausted I am, and head for home.

As the week proceeds, it seems set apart in time from the rest of my life, even set apart from my breast cancer. There's comfort in this time at home; it's the grown-up version of staying home from school, with TV, books, ginger ale, and ice cream. Now I lounge with novels, tea, and Vivaldi. Zach and Molly are thrilled that I am not at work when they go off to school. These glorious mornings, when the early spring light fills our bedroom, I am reminded of those two springs when Molly and Zach were born. I nursed each of them here in bed with me. Zach spent his first few days of life in a bassinet by the window, absorbing the sunlight as a cure for his mild case of jaundice. I feel so lucky to have nursed them, and even more to have them. How would I do this without them?

Each morning I take time to shower, letting the water run gently over my chest. Gradually, I can bear looking at my breasts, but my sense of loss is profound. One breast is higher than the other, or, to be exact, the budding, implanted breast on the left side sits higher than the real breast on the right side. I fill the left side of my bra with an old stocking and try to adjust my bra so that my clothes fit right. I change the water for the flowers and talk on the phone. I feel rested and not depressed. All my energy is focused on getting better, not on work and responsibilities. And I continue to take a respite from the decision about chemotherapy and thoughts about what will happen next.

On Wednesday I visit with Laurie, who is back at work after her recovery from a hysterectomy. Because of a suspicious screening test and a family history of ovarian cancer, Laurie was worried, but the surgeon discovered only fibroids. We talk about the other member of our study group whose biopsy revealed a ductal carcinoma in situ—that is, a lesion in the duct that could grow into cancer. She is planning a trip to California, where she will meet with Dr. Susan Love and sort out how to proceed. It is hard to believe that two of the six of us have breast cancer.

I enjoy the extra time with Molly and Zach in the afternoons. In the evenings we rent some movies. Because they see me recovering from the surgery, they think breast cancer is behind me. I continue to bask in the bountiful attention of my family and friends and to feel stronger and more resilient. But this is the honeymoon of my illness, I suspect; I've been married to a disease like this before, and I know how quickly the marriage can turn sour. Cancer is a miserable partner, and its treatment of me will be destructive and ruthless; there will be no negotiating and, like a battered wife who feels she cannot leave, I will stay for the abuse, believing that even this is better than the alternative.

Chapter four

On the Verge

My appointment with Dr. Moore is for Friday, May 7, at 4:30. On our way to the East Side, David and I talk about the money we are spending on cabs. He suggests that I not worry and consider these costs part of my medical expenses. An hour each way on buses to my appointments would do me in. When I had Hodgkin's disease, I traveled daily from Cambridge to Boston in a jitney that transported students from Harvard Yard, across the bridge over the Charles River, and into Boston to the Medical School. Generally I waited forty minutes for the bus and then tried not to vomit during the bouncy ride. From the bus I walked one-half mile across the Medical School campus to the hospital. In the waiting room of the radiology department, I waited for as long as three hours. Doing this five days a week for twelve weeks of radiation treatments was equivalent to holding a part-time job. How do people with full-time jobs, families, cancer, and little money possibly manage?

The grapevine reports that Dr. Moore is wonderful. I worried whether she would have time to see me, and I imagine she is accommodating me out of deference to Dr. Cody. Of course, she would probably see me without his referral—I must like the idea that they're taking care of me together.

David and I find our way to her office in New York Hospital and enter a rather nondescript waiting room where I give my name to the receptionist. A few old magazines are scattered about; a bulletin board is filled with notices about events relating to breast cancer. A hall leads to a number of offices, but it seems that exchanges between doctors, technicians, and secretaries happen very much out in the open here. A central space is crowded with desks, each stacked high with papers. Patients pass through and chat with the staff. I feel less like being on a blind date here than waiting to be adopted.

Soon a lively woman with curly blond hair that has begun to turn gray speaks to the receptionist, notices us, and casually introduces herself as Dr. Moore. She shakes our hands warmly. I am surprised at how she looks, although I cannot say how I imagined her. She tells us she will be with us in a few minutes, and, in fact, she soon returns to escort us to her office; how different from being led there by a receptionist. She seats us not in front of her desk but at a round table to which she pulls up a stool for herself. Just like a kitchen table, so we are equals here, though her stool is slightly higher than our chairs. She tells us that she has spoken with Dr. Cody and read my reports. She finds a pad to take down some information, and she puts on the half glasses that hang on a chain around her neck. She inquires about my children and responds to my worry about them by maintaining that children are pretty resilient in these situations. I gratefully take in this first gift from her, these words I will use to calm myself. She inquires about how I am feeling after the mastectomy, acknowledging its significance without making it too big a deal. Because she has asked about me, my emotions run very close to the surface and threaten to erupt at any moment.

David and I begin to assume our roles with her. This time I do most of the talking, though I feel young and a bit inarticulate; he is rather quiet and, even after a relationship of twenty years, this surprises me when it happens. I think of him as big, noisy, and knowledgeable and expect to hear more from him in this meeting. But I am in charge today, perhaps because this is my disease, perhaps because he is sometimes quieter and I more talkative than I generally think. I glance at Dr. Moore's credentials on the wall. She is a graduate of Smith College and Columbia University medical school, so I assume that she is upper class and Protestant. She must be about fifty. But she is at that point in middle age when she could look older or younger at any moment. Her glasses make her look grandmotherly, but she treats me as an equal; she strikes me as being someone with whom I could be friends. I imagine she makes everyone feel this way. She speaks with the authority of an accomplished professional. I like that she becomes in my mind whomever I need—a peer, a mother, a grandmother, a competent doctor.

She tells us that she would like to review my pathology report with us as a way to sort out the question of chemotherapy. She takes a piece of paper and draws a line down the middle, labeling one side positive and the other negative. In the positive column she writes, first, that the tumor is small, 1.7 centimeters, probably a little smaller in reality, as Dr. Cody said. Second, the cell type is not the best and not the worst. I'm beginning to think of this as a diagnostic category, used by all doctors for my cell type. Dr. Moore lists the cell type under the positive column, though I'm not sure why and I still don't ask. Third, my lymph nodes are all negative. Because the mastectomy removed all of the breast tissue on that side, my situation looks very good. One could make a convincing argument that chemotherapy is not necessary.

On the other hand, she continues, chemotherapy would boost my survival rate by three or four percentage points. Although some women choose not to go through chemo for such a small margin of improvement, others want to gain the increased margin if they can, especially if they have children. This is a discussion about what sort of chances I want to take with my life, and having children makes it simple: I will take no chances. But if I had no children I would be considering how much I would fight for my own life.

Now we turn to the negative side of the equation. It is likely that chemotherapy will cause a premature onset of menopause. Because of my breast cancer, estrogen replacement therapy is probably not an option, she tells me. Great, I think. Finish chemotherapy and move right into menopause without any of the relief from symptoms that estrogen provides. I recall my mother's years of hot flashes, and I know that being of slight build and northern European descent already increases my risk for osteoporosis. If I get through this cancer, I'll be a prematurely hunched over little old lady whose bones break easily. Still, that would be a small price to pay for my life.

I'm particularly worried about the side effects of chemo. I ask Dr. Moore about the long-term effects, and I explain that I have always suspected that radiation caused my hearing loss and possibly this breast cancer as well. She understands my wariness of breast cancer treatments and assures me that follow-up studies of people treated with the drugs I would be given indicate no increased risk of other cancers over a twenty-five-year period. "Could chemotherapy be repeated if I had a recurrence?" I ask. "Yes," she replies, "you could do this protocol again, if necessary." I comment that chemotherapy in my situation seems to imply a belief that breast cancer is a systemic disease; she agrees that this is the premise. I know that this notion will sway me, that I will not rest if I have not treated this potentially systemic disease systemically. It does not escape me, however, that my body may already be free of cancer cells or left with a number small enough to be handled by my immune system, in which case the chemotherapy would not be necessary. I'll never know.

Dr. Moore presents the question of chemotherapy as being my decision, but she lets me know that she will make a recommendation. She is still waiting for the results of the estrogen-receptor test. Because chemotherapy interferes with estrogen production, it is more likely to be effective if my tumor is estrogen receptive. This test is not generally of great significance, but in my case a little more information might push us one way or the other.

Dr. Moore explains that the chemotherapy routinely used for stage-one breast cancers is CMF, a combination of three drugs—Cytoxan, methotrexate, and 5-fluorouracil (5FU). CMF is generally given according to one of two schedules: on the first and eighth day of a four-week cycle or in a slightly higher dosage once every three weeks. Statistically, there seems to be no difference in the outcome of the two regimes, but Dr. Moore is more accustomed to the older, four-week regimen and it would give me slightly more chemo in total. I calculate twelve treatments instead of eight. Terrific.

She explains that many people do very well over a course of six months. They continue to work, perhaps feeling some nausea and tiredness the day or so after a treatment. When I describe the difficult time that I had with nausea and vomiting during my radiation treatments, she promises that she will do everything possible to help me manage. Women generally lose between 40 and 60 percent of their hair, though whether I will need a wig will probably not be clear until the second month or so. It's good to plan ahead for that possibility. She tells me this matter-of-factly, signaling that this is not something to get too worked up about. I've already developed a public stance on hair loss. I'm going to act maturely, even if I want to scream to the universe, "No, this can't happen."

David, who has been quiet, now asserts that we will do anything that is necessary to improve my chances of survival. Here we go again, I am thinking. Not only will "we" do any treatment imaginable to make me better, but "we" were not intent on saving my breast. How bizarre it must sound to Dr. Moore to hear David discuss "our" going through chemotherapy. I always wondered how Dr. Cody thought "we" could do without the breast. There is a thin line between empathically identifying with my experience and confusing mine with his. Sometimes David crosses the line.

When I had Hodgkin's disease, David developed a lump on his neck that matched my lump exactly in location and size. He worried silently for a long time, not wanting to upset me. "You can't be serious," I responded with a touch of sarcasm. The surgeon was not so cavalier. Because he could not feel a matching lump on the other side, which would have indicated that this was simply a part of David's anatomy, he had to do a biopsy. So we went to the same hospital where I had had my surgery, to the same waiting room, where David saw the same surgeon who had operated on me, on the same day of the week. The surgeon discovered that the lump was, in fact, a muscle. He surmised that David had twisted his neck so many times feeling for a lump that he had actually managed to get his muscle to mimic a tumor. It was quite a remarkable feat, but then again David is suggestible. In his reading he had come across a little-known case in which the spouse of a Hodgkin's disease patient developed the disease. So why shouldn't he? Before his German exam in graduate school, he nearly convinced his doctor that he had a brain tumor.

Dr. Moore wants to examine my breasts, so she shows me to an examining room off her office. While I undress, I notice on the wall a photograph of a harbor in a place like Cape Cod and a framed citation given to Dr. Moore for her work on the medical ethics committee. I'm glad. It confirms my sense that she is committed to good medical practice. She returns with the slides from my mammogram and views them on the screen before examining me. She comments on the neatness of my scar, and asks which plastic surgeon did the implant. I mention Dr. Breckman and indicate my annoyance with his bedside manner. "He's a good doctor," she says. I probably couldn't find a plastic surgeon I would like better. She examines my right breast and feels nothing of significance. She notices the small scar near my right nipple where Dr. Cody did the biopsy. She's glad to hear that the biopsy showed no signs of cancer. I tell her that I worry about that breast anyway. "This is your second cancer," she says, "Of course you worry."

After the exam we return to her office and she suggests that we think over the question of chemo this week. There's no big rush. I mention my plan to obtain a second opinion. "Of course," she says, "perhaps we should meet after that and pool all our information. It's always good to have more people considering your situation." She's so professional, so confident. By then she'll have the results of the estrogen-receptor test and be ready to make a recommen-

dation. Thank God. Although this is ultimately my decision, I appreciate that she will not leave me completely
alone with it.

We stand up, shake hands, and walk with her to the
front desk. She tells us about a conference she is attending
in Washington to discuss President Clinton's health plan. I
manage to converse, but I still feel like a needy little girl,
certainly not like a professional woman myself. She asks
about my work and suggests that I proceed slowly; women
often crash a few weeks after a mastectomy. She's named
what's begun to happen to me—crashing. Although I
bounced back after the surgery, I've been feeling much
more frightened and out of control. I could fall apart right
here with this doctor who, like a good mother, articulates
the experience that I have not been able to describe. She
tells me that her patients who are psychotherapists seem to
run on a very tight clock, always checking their watches to
make it to their next appointments. They worry more
than they need to about their patients, she says. She's
got my number again. Patients do well. Children do well.
Although not completely convinced, I take her advice as
permission to withdraw some of my energy from others
and focus more of it on myself.

回

In my week off, I wrestle with how to discuss my breast
cancer with my patients when I return to work next
Monday. My mind refuses to grapple with this, and I'm

astounded to find myself feeling more anxious about telling my patients than I did about telling my own children. With Molly and Zach there was no question of whether to tell them; they would have known that something serious was wrong. And won't my patients know? They'll see my wig if I need one. They'll sense my physical state and my feelings. In talking to colleagues, I learn of psychoanalysts so committed to the concept of the analyst's anonymity that they actually go through treatment, wig and all, without telling their patients. Although I know I couldn't pull that off, I sometimes think that I should find a way to keep my crisis to myself, to protect my patients and maintain the illusion that I will never abandon them. I come to the conclusion that telling my patients is the right thing to do and I'll have to live with the fact that I'm not following the rules. I will tell them, except for a teenaged girl who has just begun to see me; she will be at camp for the summer and this information can wait. It seems disrespectful, even damaging, to pretend to my patients that something so threatening and probably obvious is not happening. And we would miss the opportunity to discuss openly their feelings about illness and death, their fears of abandonment.

Most of them are stunned, saddened, frightened for me. Some tell me that they are relieved to know the nature of my surgery, that they had guessed breast cancer or imagined a worse cancer. They had been worried about me during my time away from work and were grateful to receive my call telling them that the surgery went well and that I'd see them as planned. They had struggled with how to communicate their concern, whether to send a card or flowers or a gift. Some did, some didn't. Many tell me how appreciative they are of my sharing this personal information. What if I had not told them and then something happened to me? They would have felt betrayed and resentful about never having had an opportunity to say goodbye.

After our initial sessions I relax and can hear more about their fears of loss and death, their anger that this has happened. Many worry about how they will talk to me about their problems if I have chemo; they won't want to impose on me. Others fear that I will be distracted and unavailable. I say that I will continue sessions, as I hope to, only if I feel I can do my work. Some of my female patients whose mothers had breast cancer tell me that they expect to get the disease themselves and are not surprised about me. They describe their mothers' illnesses and scars but often avoid their most painful feelings. Not everyone. One woman misses work and cries for days, less for me than for her mother after whose death she could not shed a tear. I am quite astounded at the high number of my patients who lost a parent at an early age. I hope they do not lose me, and I hope my children will be spared the trauma that has so affected these patients' lives.

By my third visit to Dr. Breckman I know the routine. At his office on Fifth Avenue the receptionist buzzes me in and I push hard to open the heavy, metal door. While I wait, I read slick, expensive magazines or I watch the other patients and try to determine the nature of their problems. I am usually called by one particular nurse, who listens well and answers my questions much more completely than the doctor. She offers good advice: to prevent a yeast infection while on antibiotics, take acidophilus tablets or try a course of Gyne-Lotrimin; to fill out your bra until the expander is fully inflated, use a shoulder pad. We talk about her upcoming wedding as she gets things ready for my procedure.

Dr. Breckman comes in and checks on the amount of saline he has previously injected. He tells sexist jokes about nurses while he searches for the valve that he placed under my skin during surgery, and then inserts the needle. I feel the pressure as more saline fills the expander. It's strange to have a different-sized breast every week. He asks if it hurts and coaxes me to let him insert a little more. He doesn't push hard, assuring me that he can complete the inflation in ten or twelve visits. It's up to me. I have him stop at fifty-five cubic centimeters. He then asks if I had pain after the last injection, and I report only discomfort that day; I never need more than a Tylenol. I make an appointment for the next week.

I'm still agonizing over the question of chemotherapy. David really leaves this one to me. I can't stand the thought of these treatments, but how can I forego a chance to kill off some more cancer cells if they are there? Nevertheless, I fear taking such powerful chemicals when at best they will improve my chances of survival only slightly. Even though I've been assured otherwise, I worry that they may cause permanent damage. I want all this to be over with. Why can't surgery be enough? Why must I endure six months of treatments, sickness, and humiliation? But how can I not do this for the sake of Molly and Zach? And I need insurance against feeling responsible should I have a recurrence.

On Tuesday David and I have dinner with friends and I share with them my dilemma about whether to have chemo. The woman in the couple would not. She has seen friends go through these treatments and she could not stand it. Why is she telling me this? Would she not go through chemotherapy herself for her two sons? Her husband keeps repeating that we should follow my doctors' advice because doctors know best. He ignores that mine is a borderline situation and that the doctors are not claiming to know what's best.

David talks later about how he always thought, perhaps naively, that the real task with serious illness was to find a good physician. I have good doctors, but I still need to become educated and make decisions. It seems doubly unfair. Isn't suffering from cancer enough? Why must I simultaneously make the most difficult decisions of my life?

On Wednesday I receive in the mail from a friend a book, published by Wedgestone Press, titled *One Answer to Cancer: An Ecological Approach to the Successful Treatment of Malignancy* by William Donald Kelley, D.D.S., M.S. A dentist? I browse through the testimonials from people with incurable cancers who claim to have been cured by this approach. I begin to wonder why I have chosen such a noxious treatment as chemotherapy; perhaps a change in diet or some nutritional supplements could cure me. I turn to Kelley's introduction and read his story. After various treatments for muscle aches, pains in his chest, and depression, his frustrated physician sat him down and told him there was nothing wrong with him; it was only in his mind. After some time Kelley returned to this physician with further complaints. His doctor prescribed more tests and found nothing but sent him to a specialist who suggested a biopsy of the pancreas. This suggestion shocked Kelley and convinced him that he had cancer, though he does not mention whether he ever had the biopsy. He did, however, give himself a biochemical test for the early detection of cancer—a test that doctors have found unreliable and have stopped using because it detects cancer when no other clinical signs are present. For Kelley this simply meant that the test identified cancer early, before any tumor appeared. He gave the test to his wife, his mother, and his three children, all of whom, except one child, turned out to have cancer according to this test.

In retrospect Kelley believes he failed to heed the early warning signs of cancer—gas, weakness of the eyes, tiredness, muscle weakness, changes in hair texture or color, hernias, and depression (as characterized by loss of interest in one's work). Funny, everyone I know has some of these early warning signs. Cancer, Kelley explains, simply indicates an active pancreatic enzyme deficiency, and his book purports to explain this deficiency scientifically, though it leaves me longing for some peer-reviewed and controlled studies. Cancer can generally be cured by using enemas to detoxify the body, taking nutritional and vitamin supplements now available in New York from Dr. Nicholas Gonzalez, who has carried on Kelley's work, and maintaining a proper spiritual attitude. Not everyone has a proper attitude, he points out. So not everyone will be cured? I think I'll stick to chemo.

If I do have chemotherapy, I already know that I want to work with Dr. Moore. But getting a second opinion is the responsible thing to do, or at least it is what everyone expects me to do. In New York that means an appointment at Sloan-Kettering's Breast Center. Dr. Larry Norton, the director, seems to be highly respected but is too busy to take new patients. It's Thursday and I have an appointment instead with his associate, Dr. Klauber. David accompanies me. The Breast Center, hidden away on East Sixty-fourth Street, is well endowed and provides a wide spectrum of services for women who have breast cancer. Its interior decorating is reportedly state of the art. I arrive for the appointment and am moved along from desk to desk to fill out forms and supply insurance information. A large waiting area with plush carpets and comfortable couches and chairs, all in muted colors, is warmly lit. No glaring fluorescent lights here. And the staff is very pleasant. This is the place to be. So why do I feel as if I'm on a conveyor belt?

There are many women in the waiting room, all of them under fifty, and of normal weight. They shouldn't have breast cancer, according to the conventional wisdom that says older or overweight women are the ones at risk. It also says that a woman is more at risk if breast cancer runs in her family, but in fact only a very small percentage of women with breast cancer have a family history of the disease. The women talk casually with one another and would certainly include me in their conversation. But do I want to talk? I am a newcomer to this world, and this is an initiation I'd rather avoid. An attractive, dark-haired woman in her forties who observes me waiting anxiously engages me in conversation, telling me about her first two rounds of chemotherapy. She feels tired but she is working. After her last treatment she managed a six-hour car ride to visit friends in Syracuse. Her hair is thinning but still looks fine. She assumes I'll be having chemo and tells me to drink plenty of fluids. She indicates a room with a small refrigerator full of drinks where I can get some juice. I then meet a forty-five-year-old woman whose tumor was five centimeters wide when discovered by mammography. She's wearing a great wig. She takes two days off after chemotherapy treatments but could even work those days, she claims. The third woman I meet, the mother of a three year old, had not had a mammogram. If she had, her breast cancer could probably have been discovered earlier; it is now in her bones and in an advanced stage. Why is there even a question about mammograms for women in their forties?

On the way to Dr. Cody's office last week I bought the May/June 1993 issue of *Ms.*, in which all of the articles are about breast cancer. Like the *Times*, *Ms.* reports on studies that indicate no statistical increase in rates of survival among women in their forties who have mammograms. *Ms.* also discusses the conflicting opinions on the value of mammograms. But I'm not satisfied. However balanced the reporting, all I want is a long article expressing outrage at the undervaluing of mamograms, pointing out that many women in their forties have had tumors that were detected early. I already know ten women in this situation. Perhaps this fact is not statistically significant, but I can guarantee that it is personally significant to these women, and I worry that the real underlying pressure against mammograms is that they, and biopsies, are costly.

This issue of *Ms.* also highlights the angry, political response of many women to breast cancer. Some women choose not to wear a wig and to appear bald in public as a statement that breast cancer is a reality not to be hidden. Others decide against breast reconstruction after a mastectomy and let themselves be seen with one breast. I consider myself a feminist who believes in political action. So why am I put off by this public movement? I doubt that I could proudly show my scars or my bald head. I feel sad, not proud. I'm trying to mourn my losses and accept the damage that has been done to my body. I need to do this in private, and wigs and reconstruction may afford some privacy.

As I sit in the Breast Center and talk to these women, I find myself admiring how well they have hidden what they are going through. I realize that this is what I aspire to—looking as if everything is fine. But maybe this effort to appear to be fine, to wear wigs and breast prostheses, does in fact contribute to the invisibility of breast cancer. Maybe we should be showing the world, by refusing to cover up our disease, how numerous we are and how many more resources are needed to do something about this disease.

The next woman I meet is angry—angry at her doctor, at the Breast Center, and at her brother, a physician, who insists that she come here, the "best place," even though she has her own doctor, whom she trusts, at another reputable hospital. She tells us tales of long waits and of doctors not returning calls as she struggles to decide whether to have chemo, knowing it will probably make her infertile.

David and I wait for three hours to see Dr. Klauber, and, because we'll be so late, we call and make arrangements with Eve, our babysitter, for the children to be dressed and taken to Zach's spring orchestra concert. I'm furious. Never has a doctor kept me waiting this long. Finally, we meet Dr. Klauber, a rather overweight, taciturn man who makes no apology for the delay. He takes my history, tries to impress us with his knowledge, and talks patronizingly of Dr. Moore, though she is clearly more experienced than he. Given the arrogance of the medical profession, how did I ever find Dr. Cody and Dr. Moore? In the course of the physical exam, Dr. Klauber learns from me that I took birth control pills for a short time, and he nods knowingly, as if he's identified the cause of this cancer. I wonder why, if he knows about this suspected link, he hasn't hired a public relations firm? Besides, I know that the studies linking birth control pills and cancer are inconclusive at this point, and that much depends upon a woman's age when she took the pill, the length of time she was on it, and the dosage and combination of hormones.

I return to Dr. Klauber's office and he then disappears. I talk with David, who totally dislikes him. Ten minutes later, Dr. Klauber returns. He remains standing, as if he has an important announcement to make. He tells us that he has just met with a colleague and they agree that, of course, I should have chemotherapy; anyone with a tumor larger than one centimeter should.

There's something else he must tell me, he adds, with what strikes me as a gloating demeanor. "Because of your history of Hodgkin's disease," he says, "we would highly recommend a second mastectomy before you begin further treatment." I am stunned. I look at David for his reaction but cannot read him. "Why?" I ask. "Well, there really are no studies of the incidence of breast cancer among Hodgkin's disease survivors, but we saw one woman last week who developed a cancer in one breast and had a pre-cancerous condition in the other." I point out that when my right breast was biopsied the tissue was clean, as was my mammogram and my physical exam. "Yes," he replies, "but the cancer could be hiding in some part of the breast that was not biopsied." So we should cut off my breast because I might someday develop cancer? Perhaps every-one with even a slight risk qualifies for a mastectomy.

I try to remain calm and sound rational, though my emotional barometer registers shock. This suggestion leaves me feeling panicked, as if my prognosis is worse than I thought. Why else would these doctors feel that my first-stage breast cancer needs to be clobbered, and I with it? Nothing seems enough: not a mastectomy, not chemo-therapy, and probably not a second mastectomy. Why is this doctor alarming me so? And why did the other doctors reassure me?

I ask Dr. Klauber to give me again the rationale for a second mastectomy. Well, you had radiation in both breasts. If you got cancer in one, you might get cancer in the other.

Yes, but I had much more radiation at the site of the tumor, nearer my left breast than my right. I lose track of my thinking. My mind races from one thought to another. This is Sloan-Kettering. If they say I need another mastectomy, how can I not follow their recommendation? Haven't I been secretly tortured by this question? Then again, Sloan-Kettering is known for recommending the most radical treatments, sometimes more radical than necessary. But they may have reason, given the number of women they see die of breast cancer. And Dr. Klauber did say they are glad that we Hodgkin's patients have been kept alive this long. Why lose us now? I begin to have a curious feeling of relief. Dr. Klauber is reminding me that I could get cancer again. He's offering me a recommendation that fits with my old, magical solution of cutting off offending and potentially offending body parts. Perhaps it is a good idea. I think about my patients. How can I take off again for an operation? If I need to I will. Dr. Klauber tries to reach Dr. Cody, but he's gone home for the day. I'll call him tomorrow to set up a date for surgery next week.

We rush uptown to Zach's orchestra concert and arrive at intermission. Our friends David and Zina, who have come to hear their daughter perform, see on my face the traces of my anxiety and fear. In their warm embrace I begin to cry, shaking as my effort to hold my desperation inside fails. Molly sees me crying and her face crumbles as she runs over to me. I sense her fragility immediately, and I rally, desperately, to save her from seeing more of my raw pain, much as any mother rallies when she sees her child in danger. I hold her in my arms, and she asks what's wrong. I tell her that I'm very upset about the medicine I will have to take because it will make me feel sick for a couple of months, but I'll be fine. With my arm around her I stroke her hair until she relaxes enough to go off with her friends, but I can't stop thinking about her terrified little face.

Because I'm tied up the next morning with patients, David calls Dr. Cody to make plans for surgery. Dr. Cody is astounded by Sloan-Kettering's recommendation and makes it clear that he strongly disagrees. Despite my dislike of Dr. Klauber, I had accepted his advice concerning what I must do, numbly acceded to the next terrible trial, relieved to be rid of all breasts. I spent last evening adjusting to the idea of another surgery, convincing myself that I manage surgery well and bounce back quickly. Dr. Cody's disagreement is another blow. Now what do I do? Two opposing medical opinions seem worse than a mastectomy; they mean that I will have to make a decision, not simply follow orders. Dr. Cody realizes that David and I are very upset and suggests that we drop by his office the next afternoon before my appointment with Dr. Moore. When we see him, he's angry enough to let us know his feelings about the situation. He thinks the doctors at the Breast Center are under enormous pressure to make quick diagnoses. Dr. Cody simply cannot find any basis for their recommendation other than one anecdotal case. He repeats that the mammogram of my other breast showed nothing; that my breast exam indicated no problems; and that the biopsy of tissue from my right breast showed no cancerous or precancerous cells. Of course he will watch that breast, but with no indication of a problem he cannot justify a mastectomy.

In addition, it does not make sense to delay the beginning of my chemotherapy, and another mastectomy right now would do that. We know that I had a cancer in my left breast and it's important to begin the chemotherapy, which we all are now in agreement about. In a way the discussion of a second mastectomy, because it seems such an extreme recommendation, leaves me feeling as if chemo is the least I can do in the way of further treatment.

I try to explain that, all this aside, I am now left with an impossible decision. If I decide not to have the second mastectomy, I will continue to worry. If I go ahead with it, I face another surgery with the ever present possibility of complications, with weeks of recovery and decisions about another implant, and with a delay in beginning chemo, all for possibly no reason. Dr. Cody understands my dilemma. The fact that I've had cancer in one breast increases the odds slightly of a tumor developing in the other breast; he will be checking my other breast closely through regular exams and mammograms. Any problem will likely be found early. If at a later date it seems appropriate or if I find that I cannot live with the worry, I may then decide to have a second mastectomy.

I feel at a loss. I trust Dr. Cody and know that I will go along with his recommendation, but now I have this albatross of anxiety around my neck. How will I get rid of the worry? I even wonder how I might persuade Dr. Cody to do a second mastectomy. I would probably cut off my arms and legs if someone suggested it, and Sloan-Kettering's recommendation seems headed in that direction. Finally I decide against another mastectomy; I will go along with Dr. Cody's recommendation only if he agrees to watch me like a hawk so that any sign of cancer can be detected early.

We meet with Dr. Moore at half past four. Today I am not soothed by her voice. Even more than I, David needs to vent his outrage about Sloan-Kettering. Dr. Moore listens sympathetically but doesn't join in his anger. She agrees with Dr. Cody that there is no reason to assume a problem in the second breast. The doctors at Sloan-Kettering are very good doctors. She knows Dr. Klauber; he's worked in her office and he is very bright. I wonder why she doesn't comment on his bedside manner. She spoke to him after my call earlier today, and he said that he was only suggesting that we consider a second mastectomy, clearly backing away from the statement I saw him write in my file: "We strongly recommend a second mastectomy."

I quickly add that Sloan-Kettering's opinion that I should proceed with chemotherapy did help me in reaching a decision to do so. She agrees with my decision and informs me that the results of my estrogen-receptor test are positive, a good sign for the effectiveness of the treatment. She suggests that I begin next week. We settle on the first two Fridays of each four-week cycle as the day for the treatments so that I can recover on the weekend before work on Monday. I should set up an appointment with Marta, the nurse who will work with me. She likes to spend some time with patients in advance to discuss the effects of the medications and ways of coping with them.

In the evening, David and I work out a plan for the kids during my chemo treatments. Dinner will be simple or we'll order take-out meals. I will try to be with them at dinner and in the early evening to help with their homework and music practice. When I need to go to bed, David will take over and put them to bed. I tell him that I fear that this treatment will wear us down completely. With appointments, naps, nausea, and early bedtime, I am going to be far less available. David will be assuming the endless errands that I usually do, taking over even more of the care of the children. He is going to get tired out himself. We decide to ask Eve for some help.

Eve agrees to come on Thursdays to spend a few hours with Molly—playing games, drawing, and helping her with homework. Molly loves Eve, and she can certainly use the additional attention, given that David and I are so distracted. At sixteen, Eve is becoming a lovely young woman. Her generosity is wonderful, but I'm also aware that we are bringing her into this world of ours that includes cancer. She will see how the chemo affects me— whether I lose my hair, gain weight, or look gaunt. How could it not frighten her? As the oldest child in my family, I sometimes felt that I knew too much. When my mother had a miscarriage, I helped out, but I was frightened and alone with what I imagined was happening to her, with my feelings of loss about the baby, and with my inflated sense that I had to be responsible for my siblings. I'm concerned that Eve will worry and feel too responsible. Her mother assures me that she will take care of talking with Eve.

I resent the amount of time and energy that coping with the effects of chemo will take. I love to go to the country, to have the house full of friends, sharing meals and conversations while the kids run in and out, but I doubt that I'll have the stamina. I had looked forward to conversations with my two sisters who are pregnant, but now I will barely manage to keep track of their development.

Many times in the past few years I have said to David, "Thank God no one close to me is sick or dying; I don't have time to care for anyone." Now I am the one who is sick. I have no time for an illness that so aggressively forces itself to center stage, demanding all my attention and pushing my family and friends out of the way.

It is a sunny, spring day, two weeks since my mastectomy, and I feel stronger and healthier. Our friends David and Dinitia are preparing for the bar mitzvah of their twin sons on Saturday. We learned this week that they plan to seat us at lunch with people we might find interesting— David with some science editors and me with some literary people. I find myself panicking at the thought of even one meal with people I do not know. How can I make small talk when all I can think of is cancer? How will I keep from losing my grip on the rules of social etiquette, from telling these strangers the intimate details of my mastectomy? I will feel exposed and they uncomfortable. I call Dinitia who arranges for us to sit with close friends.

The ceremony is very long and in Hebrew. The boys do their readings and maturely present their commentaries. I focus on a point implicit in their talks: that their coming of age has meant embracing Judaism and consequently rejecting Christianity. I am disturbed that they, in adopting the religion of their father, reject the background of their mother. Dinitia herself is not bothered by this; she doesn't identify strongly with her parents' tradition and shares the Judaic values of her husband. I realize that I am upset not by the twins' rejection of their mother's heritage but by the possibility that my children will overlook me, that they'll identify only with their father. I am afraid I will die and be forgotten by them.

After the service we walk up West End Avenue toward the restaurant on 107th Street, behind all the children, who are exuberant about shedding their good behavior. I chat with Marsha and Richard on the way. Marsha has been solicitous and supportive, calling with the names of friends I might contact who have had breast cancer. Richard listens to me with understanding. He tells me how worried they were when Marsha had a biopsy. At our table I join Pam and Roger, whom I have not seen since they visited me in the hospital. Roger inquires jokingly about my mental health, but I appreciate the seriousness of his question.

I am grateful to these men for not being afraid to talk to me about my breast cancer. A number of my close male friends have let their wives speak to me for them. Some haven't mentioned my cancer even when they see me face to face. I suppose they are imagining my breast that isn't there, conjuring up the empty space, as I did when I visited Jan after her mastectomy. I'm angry and hurt that these men do not find a way to acknowledge my pain, but at least they don't literally flee. Last week an acquaintance with cancer told me about running into a friend on the street. The friend immediately ran away from her, toward a cab, while shouting, "I haven't called you because I just can't handle it."

Seated at my table is a science editor at the *New York Times*. We talk about our children and then about her work. I soon launch into an emotional critique of the reporting by the *Times* on the studies that suggest no increased benefit to women in their forties from mammography screening. Why didn't the *Times* give greater emphasis to the arguments of those who still favor testing women in their forties? I try to sound rational but am vaguely aware that I may lose my grip. Nevertheless, sensing that she is sympathetic to my point of view, I pick up steam. I tell her about all the women I have met whose cancers were diagnosed through a mammogram. I go on and on, vaguely aware that my behavior is inappropriate. This is not a polite topic for a bar mitzvah lunch. But I've cornered this woman and won't let her go, even if she had nothing to do with the article. She kindly listens. I like her and wish I could allow us room to get to know each other.

It is Tuesday, May 18, and I am meeting with Marta to discuss the details of chemotherapy. Marta is Panamanian and very beautiful. She carries herself with consummate dignity and radiates warmth and intelligence. She has a young daughter whom she clearly adores. Marta explains that, as a team, she, Dr. Moore, and the other nurses will do everything they can to help me through these treatments. She views chemotherapy in a positive light, as a very powerful weapon against cancer. She explains that the drugs used in chemotherapy interfere with the process of cell division in cancer cells, causing the cells to die. Because different drugs interrupt this process at different points, she tells me, I will be given more than one kind of drug. Chemo acts on all rapidly dividing cells—bone marrow cells as well as cancer cells—so they space out the treatments in order to give the bone marrow time to recover. The goal is to decrease cancer cells in the body to a number that the immune system can handle.

The three drugs referred to as CMF will be given in different steps. Methotrexate and 5-fluorouracil (5FU) will be given intravenously on each of the first two Fridays of the cycle; during those two weeks I will take the Cytoxan in pill form three times a day. Then for two weeks I will have no treatment so that my body can recover. My blood cell counts will be taken before each treatment and again about ten days after the second one. The white cell counts are important in regulating the chemo. On the twelfth day of the cycle, I will be most susceptible to infection and should avoid contact with large crowds or people who are sick. If my counts have not come back up by the next treatment, it can be delayed a day or two without compromising its effectiveness. Marta shows me a diagram of the one-month cycle that she is describing.

The major side effect is nausea. Fortunately, there are some new, more effective drugs for counteracting it. The team will work with me to adjust the type and dosage of antinausea medication to help me manage. Generally, people have some reaction to the chemo for a day or two after each treatment, but I may be able to function normally most of the time. I tell Marta, as I tell everyone, how little relief I had from the nausea related to my radiation treatments for Hodgkin's disease, but I do feel encouraged by her optimism. I realize now, sitting here, how little attention the radiologists in Boston paid to helping me manage the side effects.

Marta suggests that I stock up on bland foods such as bagels and potatoes and that I avoid spicy foods. Because I may be tired, I should rest and let others help me out as much as possible. She adds, quite to the point, that I must focus on getting better for my children, even if it means being less available to them in the short run.

She tells me that some people find it helpful to listen to music or a meditation tape while the chemo is being administered. She suggests that I imagine the chemicals attacking the cancer cells, that I cooperate with rather than fight the chemo. I can predict that I'll fail at this task. I'm the kind of person who registers every irritation, who is bothered by someone smoking at the opposite end of a room, by noise in the background, by lettuce that is brown at the edges. It's hard to imagine not loathing every minute it takes these chemicals to enter my body. Besides, I'm skeptical about the efficacy of a positive attitude. Why not be honest about one's misery? Yet Marta is beautiful and encouraging; she makes me want to try.

According to Marta, some people experience an odd, metallic taste in their mouths from the chemo. Sucking on Lifesavers or hard candy usually helps. Some develop mouth sores; if I do, I should call the office right away. Because my hair is likely to become very dry, I might consider using conditioner. I will probably lose hair, and I may need to wear a wig or scarves and turbans. Marta gives me a list of places that sell wigs, including a shop run by two women who themselves had breast cancer. They also sell underwear, lingerie, and scarves. She encourages me to call her anytime; she is here to help me.

During the week we talk to Zach and Molly about chemo. I tell them again that the doctor thinks he removed all the cancer cells when he took out the tumor. I still am not specific about the mastectomy. I tell them I'm probably better already, but my doctors want to be sure by giving me some medicine that will kill any cancer cells that may remain. Because the medication has to be very strong to kill the cancer cells, it might also make me sick. "No, it's not strong enough to kill me, just strong enough to make me feel sick and maybe vomit sometimes. It will get the bad cells, but it won't get me." "Like roach killer, Mommy?" "Yes, my little New York daughter; it kills bugs but not people."

I tell them that Daddy will be doing many of the tasks we usually share—shopping, making dinner, and putting them to bed—and that I will have to take the medicine for six months, which will seem like a very long time. "But after a while you'll be all right?" asks Zach. "Yes, Zach I'll be all right." I'm beginning to see that he copes by taking the long view—that eventually I'll be better. I hope I can take that view. I assure them that, when the treatment has ended, life will return to normal.

I spend the week preparing myself by resting, taking walks, and speaking on the phone to friends about my fears. Time for everyone's anxiety again. One friend heard that tamoxifen is a drug that cures cancer and I might want to take that instead of having chemo. Another tells me that her cousin underwent an alternative treatment years ago when he had a terminal cancer diagnosis. He's now fine. "It's a shame that this method, a proven alternative to chemo, has received so little funding," she says. It's a shame that you are so insensitive, I think. Why are so many people talking about the efficacy of every treatment except the one that I am having? They must be terrified themselves of this chemotherapy, with its bad reputation. Not everyone ignores what I am feeling; many listen to my fears and withhold their own. They ask what they can do. I remember Marta's advice about accepting help. Promises of chicken, soup, and casseroles roll in.

An old friend, Michael, is passing through New York and stops by to visit with David and me. I feel anxious in talking with him because I fear that he will judge me. He's had some success with homeopathic cures and has already spoken with David on the phone about vitamin treatments for cancer. I have spent the past few weeks learning the language of breast cancer treatments—lumpectomy, radical and modified radical mastectomy, reconstruction, breast implant and reduction, chemotherapy, Cytoxan, methotrexate, and 5FU. I have come to think of my body in very concrete terms and the cancer as a determined killer out to destroy my cells. I have been steeped in the medical world's vision of attacking the cancer, of killing it before it kills me.

I have also struggled endlessly with my fears of chemotherapy. It is toxic, a poison, a killer. That is the point. I hope it will kill the cancer before it kills me. But I'm very frightened. For years I've been careful about what I eat. I avoid red meat and routinely eat fresh fruits and vegetables. I don't smoke or use drugs and I drink little alcohol. And now I am choosing to have toxic chemicals injected into my veins. I will be reminded of this toxicity every day. My hair will fall out. I will feel tired and nauseated, and I'll have a metallic taste in my mouth. I will know every minute that these chemicals are inside me, killing off parts of me—the cancer parts, I hope, and not just the other parts. Having lived through radiation treatments, I know the horror of losing my hair, vomiting, and feeling desolate.

I let Michael know my fears, hoping he will sense my conflicting emotions about chemotherapy and not add to the struggle. But sharing my vulnerability seems to have the opposite effect. He assumes that I'm open to suggestion and urges me to try vitamin therapy instead. I feel enraged and become very quiet. How do I respond to this? Is he saying that I'm foolish for choosing Western medicine when there is a cleaner, more benign cure? Would he really refuse chemotherapy treatment if faced with the decision? Didn't he go to the most reputable specialist in New York when he had medical problems? Does he truly believe that the entire medical establishment, in its arrogance, refuses to look at this "proof" of the curative properties of vitamins?

David responds calmly and says that he would be interested in seeing the studies. I know that my silence communicates annoyance, and I am critical of myself for not having found a way to be gracious and disengaged in these situations. Were I comfortable with my own decision, I would probably react less defensively. But how do I defend this grotesque decision of mine? I talk to David later about how hurt and angry I am. David is not in conflict. He feels that there is no solid, scientific evidence that these alternatives cure cancer. He reflects on the irony that he, a historian of medicine who is generally critical of the medical establishment, avidly supports medical intervention for me. He would have supported my decision for or against chemotherapy, but I know he's relieved that I have chosen this route, and his support keeps me on track.

Chapter five

The Descent

It is May 21 and I am scheduled for my first chemotherapy treatment. Our next-door neighbors, Arnhild and Paul, are planning to take Molly and Zach to the country for the weekend so that David and I will be free to cope in whatever way seems necessary. It's a good arrangement. Their sons are like older brothers to Zach and Molly. Keir is home from Swarthmore College for the summer and Colin, who is in high school, will be around as well; they're eager to help out with the kids.

Chemotherapy remains the thing I most fear will be unmanageable. Of course surgery was no picnic, but I knew I could deal with the pain and the adjustment. Constant nausea is different. I never adjusted last time. When I visit Cambridge, I still recall every place I vomited—on Cambridge Street, outside Harvard Yard on graduation day, in the middle of the reading room at Widener Library. It's not that I vomited daily, but I always felt it was a possibility, so I was ever vigilant—ready to run out of the room at any moment or to exit the bus quickly, despite the fact that I might be stranded far from home.

Sitting in Dr. Moore's waiting room, I realize that this is the most dreaded appointment since my diagnosis. Eventually I am called to have my blood taken, and after forty-five minutes Dr. Moore calls me to her office. David joins us and we sit around her table and talk. She is very matter-of-fact in her conviction that I'll get through this. She begins to write down the plan for the month—a treatment today and then again next Friday. Beginning tomorrow, I will take the Cytoxan orally, three times a day for fourteen days. I try to imagine actually swallowing these pills of my own free will, ingesting this third chemo medication, knowing it might make me sick. I will then be without treatment for two weeks, though. I will need to have my blood tested again the tenth day after my second treatment.

Now she describes the plan for today. Before my treatment she will give me a tablet of Zophran, one of the new antinausea medications. Because Zophran is still under patent, it is prohibitively expensive at nineteen dollars a pill. She checks to be sure that our insurance plan will cover the costs. I should take Zophran three times a day the first day or so and then try a combination of Zophran and Compazine, another antinausea medication. I should have some Metamucil handy because Zophran causes constipation. Finally, she writes a prescription for Ativan, an anti-anxiety medication, to help me through the first few days and insure that I sleep well.

Dr. Moore explains that she will administer the treatment herself today and begins by giving me my first Zophran tablet. She explains that she will insert a small needle into the vein on the back of my hand and will give me the methotrexate and the 5FU. This will take about ten minutes. I sit numbly through these instructions, trying to hold back the terror. Dr. Moore places my arm on a short board and wraps a rubber tourniquet around it to secure it to the board. She then finds my vein and inserts the needle. One of the chemicals is an odd, very bright yellow, not the color of anything natural, and the other is clear. How can I let her put these chemicals into me? Dr. Moore is telling me about the Washington conference she attended where she participated in a panel on breast cancer. The chemicals feel cold as they enter my body. Hillary Clinton gave an interesting speech and then left before Dr. Moore's panel presented, she tells me, with a hint of self-deprecation, as if amused at where she stands on the ladder of health policy makers. I feel the coldness of the chemicals moving through my veins, these ugly intruders I must accept into my body, supposed experts in killing cancer cells. Dr. Moore tells me what Hillary was wearing.

As I begin to relax a little, David and I talk to Dr. Moore about the weekend; we are without the children, so we'll stock up on videos. She tells me that some people go out to the movies, that one woman and her husband stayed at an inn after treatments. People often feel queasy but able to function. I'm surprised that she doesn't picture me laid up in bed all weekend. Perhaps we will go to the country sometimes. In ten minutes the treatment is finished, and Dr. Moore tells me I will not feel the effects for five or six hours. She reminds me that I can call if I have any questions and she wishes me well.

We leave the office, take the elevator down, and then exit by the rear door, passing many people who look like the walking wounded. Outside there are staff people on their breaks, vans delivering and picking up patients in wheelchairs, other patients, looking weak and leaning on their companions' arms. How different from the front entrance with its impressive lobby, uniformed guard, and nicely dressed visitors. We're the secret underclass.

I am monitoring everything I feel, waiting to see what happens. I already feel something, a little woozy, a little disoriented, perhaps just anxious. I decide to meet Molly and Zach at the bus stop in order to maintain a semblance of normal life as long as possible. David heads for the drug store to purchase the medications. I feel anxious and distracted as I wait for Zach and Molly. They bound off the bus and we walk home, they in their everyday world, I in my surreal one. I get their clothes ready for the weekend, make dinner, and send them off with Paul and Arnhild. David goes out to rent some movies for us, and I find myself wanting to lie down. I do feel nauseated but am not knocked over by it. I take an Ativan and sleep well.

On Saturday morning I feel queasy, but I'm interested in trying to act normal. We decide to visit David's parents in New Jersey, and we stop at a deli on the way so that I can satisfy my craving for a turkey sandwich. At their house we sit and talk; I am aware that David, Sophie, and Alex are watching me, as I am watching myself, to see if I begin to retch, explode, implode, faint, or shake. Nothing dramatic happens, but at about two o'clock I begin to feel tired and disoriented and so we go home. I spend the rest of the day in bed, sleeping on and off, eating bagels and doughnuts, trying to watch old movies but realizing the ones we've chosen will certainly not work—neither Fred Astaire and Ginger Rogers nor even Humphrey Bogart and Lauren Bacall can hold my interest. Next time we'll try tragedy or violence.

On Sunday Dr. Moore leaves a lovely message on my machine, hoping I am doing well. I am genuinely moved by her call. I continue to note every sensation in my body to determine the effect these chemicals are having. I become acquainted with the awful feeling of chemo, so difficult to describe—feeling sick in every limb, in every cell; feeling nauseated; seeing the world as if through a veil, slightly hazy and distorted. I hate the feeling. I drink fluids constantly, especially orange juice and ginger ale, the comfort drinks of my childhood illnesses. I sleep on and off until three o'clock when I begin to feel better; I get dressed so that David and I can walk in Riverside Park. It's a beautiful spring day, but I'm uncomfortable in the park, that other world of healthy people riding their bikes and playing ball. We don't stay long; I get hungry and we go home to make pasta while we wait for the kids to return.

I call a few friends who have left solicitous messages. Although I can report that the chemo was manageable, that I was very nauseated but did not vomit, it's harder to describe why I feel so little relief after surviving this first weekend. My internal state is too chaotic; I'm terrified all the time, if not of the chemo, by the thought of dying. How can I explain this dark fear coursing through my body along with the chemicals? How can I explain how little comfort even a good prognosis holds when you know you have cancer, when you know this killer has entered your body?

I am determined to work on Monday. I manage to see my patients despite my preoccupation with the thought of my body filled with chemicals, and I feel slightly light-headed and nauseated. Some of my patients, the ones who are keeping track, know that I have just begun chemo, and the fact that I now drink water during sessions is a reminder. When they inquire, I tell them that I had a hard weekend but felt better by Sunday. As I become absorbed in listening to them, I actually forget about the chemo. Perhaps I'm managing because it's morning and I'm rested; perhaps my concentration on my patients really does distract me—an unusual thought for someone as resistant as I am to the notion of the mind's power over the body.

I decide to look for a wig this week, assuming this to be a task better undertaken while I still feel well. I've asked my friend Pam to help me. She is the busiest person I know. She is the executive director of Bellevue, the largest public hospital in the country, and she is going through a divorce. But she generously offers to research wigs and to go with me to as many places as necessary. She approaches this task as if buying a dress—it's an adventure rather than an imposition.

We first visit Edith Imre's, a wig shop with a long tradition of helping cancer patients. We enter the second-floor "salon" on Fifty-seventh Street. Pam has made an appointment for me, so we check in with the receptionist. While waiting for Mrs. Imre, I read a book about chemotherapy that includes mention of her wigs and of the startling and horrific fact that, with chemo, women sometimes lose their eyebrows. Maybe it only happens on drugs stronger than CMF, I hope.

I try to put aside this disturbing bit of information to prepare for the present, unwanted experience. Mrs. Imre eventually ushers us into a messy office littered with unattractive wigs. She tells us that she is Hungarian and then explains to us the science of wigs in which she is expert. Human hair, which is expensive, droops in the rain and requires considerable upkeep. She recommends a combination of human and synthetic hair, which only needs to be washed gently in cold water every few weeks, then shaken out and hung to dry. She also suggests I choose a wig that's made by hand rather than machine: the weave is tighter, insuring fewer gaps through which people can see my scalp. She quickly brings her speech to an end and takes us to meet the man who will help me try on wigs.

I sit in a chair in front of a mirror while he finds a wig close in color to my hair. The wig is not yet styled; when he puts it on my head, it's huge, bushy, and atrocious. He will style it for me. I notice his crooked toupee and think, This is the man who will style my wig. As he brushes the wig into a tamer style, I begin to see a version of my hairstyle to which I could possibly adjust. Pam concurs. Still, something about the way that he's handling the wig doesn't give me confidence. Everyone who told me of having bought a wig here said that the cut never seemed right. "Do you have any prestyled wigs?" I ask, hoping to avoid spending money on a wig that would then have to be styled by his scissors. I try a wig with shorter hair, but I look frumpy. I tell him that I need to shop more before making a purchase and leave feeling that this undertaking is difficult but possible.

I suggest another place a few doors down that I had passed earlier. Who would have guessed that fashionable East Fifty-seventh Street houses a world of wigs? The wigs in the shop window look better than those at Edith Imre's, but the saleswoman's behavior is worse. Standing behind the counter, she ignores our entrance and grimaces when I ask to look at some wigs. "After I finish my lunch," she replies, "you can try on two wigs and make an appointment to try on more for $150." I'm ready to walk out, but Pam encourages me to try a few. Finally the woman, her lunch over, seats me in a chair. I again choose a wig that looks like my hair, straight and chin length, and another of shorter hair. I'm cringing inside as the saleswoman perfunctorily brushes each wig. I've never had my nails done, never had a facial or a massage. Why must I sit through this primping? The wigs look terrible and the woman is cold, as if annoyed at our imposing on her. Does she think

I'm doing this for fun? As we leave, Pam comments loudly, "This is certainly not a place to do business." I admire her confidence. I had attributed my discomfort to being more at home in Sears or J.C. Penney's than on Fifty-seventh Street. But Pam knows lack of courtesy when she sees it.

I've had enough for one day. Pam encourages me to pursue our remaining leads soon—Bits & Pieces on Columbus Avenue and a skilled transvestite hairdresser. I like the idea of someone good at playing the part. After all, isn't that really what I'm trying to do?

On my way home I recall my search for a wig when I was twenty-six. My doctors and nurses offered me no advice. Because I was a graduate student with little money, I took myself to a sale at Filene's Basement, where I tried on unstylish, synthetic wigs. The other women there seemed to resent my presence, as if I was mocking them by my youth. I hurriedly bought a wig just to escape, hung it in my room, and never wore it. Instead, I wore scarves to cover the back of my head when my hair fell out. When I first met David, I often wore scarves and jeans. He found them attractive. Little did he know what this style would come to mean for us. Now I'd look dowdy in scarves. So I'll get a wig and wear it, at least to work.

It's May 28, the day of my second chemotherapy appointment. Dr. Moore inquires about my week. It wasn't too bad, I hear myself saying; I felt pretty sick until late Sunday and then queasy until Tuesday evening. My blood counts remained so high, she says, that she's going to increase the chemotherapy dosage. So much for bouncing back quickly. My body can clearly tolerate more, and more is better; but what about my mind, I wonder. Marta administers the second treatment. Although I know I am being weaned from Dr. Moore, I feel no resentment. I know that she is with me in this, and Marta seems equally dependable.

As we leave the hospital, I notice that the other patients exiting the building are generally older than I, except one handsome man in his forties who is almost bald from chemo. He is leaning on the arm of a beautiful woman I imagine to be his wife. I am startled by a feeling of painful connection to them. I realize that I have never imagined our roles reversed—David sick and I supporting him. The thought makes me want to cry.

After my appointment I have a moment of courage and suggest to David that we stop at Bits & Pieces. We head for Columbus Avenue and discover the shop's appealing display window full of wigs and other hair pieces. I approach the desk and meet Gwen, a young man who speaks with a slight French accent; a recent immigrant, maybe. He seems eager to help. I explain that I am going through chemotherapy and may need a wig. He seats me in a chair in front of a mirror and sits down to talk with me. He tells me that with CMF I will lose only 40 to 60 percent of my hair, but I may lose my eyebrows. If that happens, he can help me with make-up tips. Such as drawing on eyebrows, I suspect. There are lighter and more comfortable wigs to wear when my hair is partially gone. Like Mrs. Imre, he suggests a wig of synthetic and human hair. As we talk, I look at many acceptable, prestyled wigs, and I notice other customers browsing. Gwen explains that people often wear wigs for fun, convenience, and diversity. You've got to be kidding, I think. But it's amusing to pretend that this is not about cancer. He points out a woman working in the shop who has long, gorgeous hair. It's impossible to tell that she is wearing a wig even though she has no bangs to hide the seam. The trick, Gwen explains, is knowing how to brush the hair piece.

He brushes my hair back and fastens it with a rubber band into a short pony tail. I look like an aging, male hippy. Then he puts a stocking cap on my head. Now I look like a burglar. If it were Halloween, this might be fun. He fits me with a wig that resembles my hair, not a full wig but one I could wear when my hair becomes thin. He describes the kind of brush to use and suggests a wig with bangs that could hide thinning eyebrows. Not those eyebrows again. I begin to see the possibilities as he brushes. He adds a scarf and I look a little like Hillary Clinton in her early, unfashionable phase. He points out that the scarf detracts from the line of the wig. David is uncharacteristically enthusiastic. He thinks I look great: "Sort of handsome, matronly," he says. He's so tactful, I think, but I love him for coming to a place that is so foreign to him. I know that, when I've managed this wig experience, I'll be able to manage my hair falling out. And I know I can cry tonight.

I buy the wig and Gwen encourages me to return if I need to have adjustments made. They also sell other products that I might want to consider: cloth turbans to wear to the beach or to bed (to hide from my husband, I think), bangs, fringes of hair to wear under hats instead of the wig. I again feel the horror that all this primping is designed to hide.

In the cab David and I make plans to pick up the kids and drive immediately to the country so that we arrive before I feel sick. We discuss my wearing the wig today so that the kids and I can get used to it. I'm finding this excruciating, but I'm determined to deal with this adjustment. When I greet Molly and Zach, I catch a brief glimmer of surprise on their faces, but this reaction never reaches their consciousness. God, I can pass. I decide to play out this charade until they notice.

On the way to the country Molly suggests that I wear a scarf like the one I'm wearing when I get my wig. David and I smile. I love the way her mind works. Zach asks how my treatment went, and I tell him that my body took the medicine so well that Anne Moore decided to give me more. Without missing a beat he says, "Anne Moore and more and more." I know her name will never again be mentioned in our home without a laugh.

We arrive at our country house and I make dinner. When I finally reveal my subterfuge, Molly and Zach are delighted by the joke and fascinated by the wig. They insist that they knew all along, as each parades through the house in it. I'm deeply touched by their acceptance of the preposterous.

I spend the rest of the weekend sleeping and eating. For me, food calms the nausea. I hate that I am alone in bed, away from David and the kids, who are busy with their friends—playing basketball, riding bikes. David comes in periodically, but I feel too miserable to visit with him. I find it uncanny that again on Sunday at about three o'clock I begin to feel better. Marta said that my reaction would fall into a pattern. I get up and we all decide to find a restaurant that serves steak, because steak is all I want. Zach can't believe it. "You're gonna eat steak?" he exclaims, delighted to see his mother break out of her chicken and fish habit. He orders steak, too. Afterward, we even manage a movie. On Monday morning, Memorial Day, some friends come by for coffee, and I feel very sick again. I lie on the couch and admit to myself that visiting during these times is too hard. Another vital part of my life cut away.

I continue to take the Cytoxan every day for two weeks. Like a good patient, I try to imagine myself sending each of the large white pills on its mission to kill cancer cells. But all I can really think about is how to get them down without gagging. I drink lots of fluids every day, glasses and glasses of water while I work. I suck on Lifesavers to mask the bad taste in my mouth. I'm also eating a lot, and my Sunday craving for red meat must be my body's signal that it needs protein or iron. When I discussed this craving with a nurse last week, she hoped I was not one of "those vegetarians" who has trouble getting enough protein. I eat doughnuts and bagels, sometimes salad, meat, vegetables. I put aside worries about weight because food helps me manage the nausea.

I am tired every day in a way that sleep does not alleviate—"chemo-tired," as I've come to call it. I resist my two-hour afternoon naps less than I did when I had Hodgkin's disease, perhaps because the time alone is less threatening now that I have a family who will be home later. As the day progresses, my ability to cope deteriorates. When

Molly and Zach return from school I struggle fairly unsuccessfully to be a good mother. I try to listen to Molly's piano practicing, but I'm completely distracted. Zach tells me about his homework assignments, but I can barely comprehend what he is saying. The children seem fine, largely because David comes home early to spend time with them and he is such a good parent. Perhaps wanting a parent for myself, I compete with them for David's attention. I need him to hear me say, again and again, every day, how sick I feel and how scared I am. It's humiliating to feel like such a child in front of him. He would never act like this.

My hair has not yet begun to fall out, and I'm trying to figure out what to do with it. Some people advise me to cut it very short to avoid the shock of losing it. But if I cut my hair short and then it becomes very thin, it may look worse. I settle on a compromise. If my hair is just a little shorter it will hang less heavily and the hair loss will be less noticeable.

It is June 3 and I have an appointment for a haircut. Although I am feeling too vulnerable to deal with the Fifty-seventh Street hair salon, where Varti, my hairdresser, is now employed, I push myself to follow through. As I sit observing women having their hair cut, dyed, or curled, panic begins to rise to the surface and I sense that I am going to fall apart, but I try to calm myself. Varti is cutting another woman's hair. I tell his assistant that I'd like to talk to him before I have my hair washed. Varti comes over, assuming, I think, that I am ready for a different style and want to discuss it. I tell him that I have breast cancer and am going to lose much of my hair. I begin to cry. He tells me not to worry, that he's sure I'll be fine. He agrees that he should cut my hair a little shorter, but not too short. By the time my hair is washed and I seat myself in his chair, I am under control again. He asks me about the diagnosis and about my kids. When my hair begins to fall out, he'll figure out how to cut it, he says.

Despite Varti's kindness, I leave hating this place, feeling humiliated. I've always felt uncomfortable among these wealthy, well-groomed women. Varti has been cutting my hair for ten years, and I have followed him from shop to shop. But I'm determined never to come here again. Why hadn't I better anticipated what it would be like here? I feel as if I have just had my final haircut. I am envious of these women and their full-bodied hair, their unencumbered leisure, their bodies that can be pampered and primped, not cut up and sewn together.

When I get home, I call my friend Laurie. Since her gynecological surgery, she has developed an enlarged node on her neck, and her doctor, uncertain of its meaning, performed a biopsy last week. She tells me now that she has been diagnosed with inflammatory breast cancer, an advanced cancer that has spread like a sheet throughout her breast. She is scheduled for a consultation at the Breast Center at Sloan-Kettering to discuss a bone marrow transplant. She assures me that she is managing fairly well and, in her typical way, inquires about me.

I'm stunned. Laurie can't have breast cancer, too, and such an aggressive, insidious kind, undetectable by a mammogram and forming no lump in her breast. My heart aches for her as I listen to the medical nightmare that the process of diagnosis has already been for her—endless doctors, long waits for phone calls, fear. I don't know what to say. I feel overwhelmed by my situation and unable to offer much in the way of encouragement. And I am excruciatingly aware of the greater danger to her. To presume that we are in the same situation would be to underestimate her difficulties. To talk about the difference would distance me from her. We talk about our children. She has a son Zach's age who will be going to camp with him.

David becomes very upset when I break the news to him. He can't believe that Laurie has been catapulted into such a nightmare. He's worried about what she must face and about her chances of surviving this. And he's astounded that three of the six women in my study group have breast cancer. Statistics say breast cancer affects one of nine women. In this group it's one of two. Of course it's a coincidence, three strokes of bad luck, but what if the laws of statistics, which I think of as regulating the occurrences of horrible experience, no longer apply? What if I'm right about statistics, that a 90 percent probability that my cancer won't recur is just a mental construct designed to keep me from going crazy? What if things are as out of control as they feel and breast cancer really can happen to anyone?

In the evening I read a letter I received from Terry, a close friend from graduate school. Terry and I, both graduates of Catholic high schools, went on to pursue doctorates at Harvard. At the time, Terry's mother had developed the breast cancer that eventually killed her. I was close to Terry as she suffered through her mother's illness. I recall that her mother complained little, struggling to keep up her appearance by dressing well and wearing make-up. It seemed to help her carry on.

Terry's reactions to my Hodgkin's disease were colored by her experience with her mother's cancer. I fondly remember two incidents. When I first told Terry about my diagnosis and followed it with my customary recitation of the 95 percent survival rate, Terry thought the survival rate doubtful. She could relate my experience only to her own reality, a world where people would die of cancer. Not psychologically astute enough at the time to understand Terry's reaction, I felt confused and hurt. Weeks later, when I was recovering from surgery, I put a "No Visitors" sign on my hospital door to give myself some rest. Terry was outraged; she burst through the door, saying, "The nurses told me you wanted no visitors, but I insisted you couldn't mean me." In a way, she was right.

Terry now writes me a loving letter, filled only with concern for me, free of the anxiety that she, when younger, could not contain. I imagine that as the daughter of a woman who died of breast cancer, she must continue to feel plenty of anxiety about her own health. I can tell from the letter that she has matured, and I'd love to spend time with her now that we're grown up.

My mother and sister Chris are planning a trip from Buffalo to visit me the weekend of June 10th when I have no chemo. I've declined my mother's repeated offers to come and help with the children, but I've told her that I really need to see her. When I had Hodgkin's disease, I asked my mother to delay visiting me until after my surgery. I later learned how helpless she felt while waiting so long. When she visited after Zach's birth, I was grateful for a second chance to let her come and take care of me. As this visit approaches, I feel increasingly upset and realize that I am pressuring myself to hide my being sick from her. I want to protect her from all of this pain. She insists that she can handle it, and I know how much she has dealt with in her life. She left school at sixteen to take care of her mother, who had Parkinson's disease and died a few months before my birth, as did her twenty-eight-year-old sister, of colitis. After raising six children, she had to cope with my sister's illness. And now this. She doesn't deserve an ounce more pain.

And my father. When Chris was in intensive care, my mother urged him to tell Chris that he loved her. It was hard for him to say the words. How can I expect this man who never talks about his feelings to do so now? My friend Gina once described visiting my parents after my Hodgkin's disease diagnosis and my father tearfully talking about me and my illness. Now he talks to me on the telephone more than he ever talked—about the family, his garden, my children; still not about his feelings, but it no longer matters.

For some reason I dwell less during this cancer on my parents' pain, even less than I did when my sister was sick. Knowing what it's like to be a parent, I cannot bear to think of the pain that my illness causes them. Nor can I now handle more pain than my own and my children's.

My mother and Chris arrive on Wednesday, and we spend the afternoon talking. I relax when I know that my mother is relieved to see me feeling well. Over dinner, David keeps saying, "Doesn't she look good? She's going to be fine." Chris and I talk about our operations like two old ladies. She shows me the zipperlike scar that runs down the front of her body. Her doctors certainly sewed her up tightly in her most recent operation. I show her my mastectomy scar. It is important to show someone, to advance from feeling grotesque and hidden to being seen and accepted.

On Thursday David takes my mother and Chris to the Metropolitan Museum while I see patients. Rather than joining them for lunch, I take a nap so that I am rested for Molly and Zach's spring violin concert in the evening. Alex and Sophie join us for dinner at the same Chinese restaurant we went to with our families the night before David and I were married.

The concert is a moving and exciting experience as always. This evening, both Itzhak Perlman and Isaac Stern are in the audience, hoping to bring publicity and financial support to this program, which New York City's Board of Education may no longer finance. I love to watch these children—all sizes, shapes, colors, and ages—play their violins together.

The graduates return for these concerts, like older children returning for family events. This school is truly integrated, the children in attendance being of every race and class. Among the parents are teachers, subway conductors, lawyers, mothers on welfare, doctors, and postal clerks. One senses the staff's commitment and love for the children. No audience can beat this one for enthusiasm.

Two years ago I cried through the spring concert, having just learned that Chris had been flown by emergency helicopter from Buffalo to the Cleveland Clinic for a possible liver transplant. I was scheduled to fly to Cleveland the next day and, as I listened to these children sing, I felt torn apart by the thought that Chris's children might lose their mother. This is what I have not allowed myself to feel about my own children. Before this cancer, the thought that I would ever become sick and die, leaving my children motherless, was unbearable. Now I cope by not allowing myself to feel that possibility in any real way, though the thought is always with me. When Chris and a friend were both very sick two years ago, I noticed that they seemed distant from concern about their children. Chris later told me that she was too sick to do more than survive. But I think it was more than that. What mother can ever imagine dying and leaving her children?

On Sunday Chris and I go for a short walk, attentive to the limits placed on her by the fluid that remains in her lungs. She is no longer my little, tag-along sister, but a grown woman who talks to me about how one goes on with life after facing the possibility of death. She offers me the wisdom she says I shared with her when she was sick— that when this is over I will become involved again in ordinary life; the fear will recede to the background. She seems to have less anger and more acceptance of her situation than I do of mine. She has always been more accepting of life's events; or perhaps, observing me, she declined the hysterical approach. I tell her two things I remember from visiting her in Cleveland: finding her reading the prayer card left for her by the priest and hearing that Jim, her husband, went to the chapel to pray. How ironic. I was always the one who insisted that the family say grace at meals and never miss Mass; she preferred less good behavior. I prayed for her when she was sick, but I don't really know how to pray for myself, to admit how much my health is out of my hands. I think of Job enduring plagues and insects patiently. Did Job believe in an afterlife? He must have, to be so patient. My friend Jane suggests I read the literature of Eastern cultures, whose people seem to have a vivid sense of the cycles of life. My friend Audrey, who had chemo, suggests the Holocaust literature.

In the last few days of this first four-week cycle, I feel ecstatic that my body has recovered. The night before my first June treatment, David and I have dinner with friends and I dominate the conversation, interested in knowing about them, encouraged to talk about myself by their admiration for how well I'm coping. As we pay the check, I take note of the feeling in the pit of my stomach that announces my fear about the next day's chemo. I feel as terrified as I did before my surgery and before my first two treatments. Will going to treatments get any easier or will I feel each time as if I am preparing for my own execution? I awaken often during the night, seized by fear. I am relieved when morning comes and I can get on with the chemo.

Chapter six

The Second and Third Cycles

This is my third trip to New York Hospital for chemotherapy. On one level the experience has become routine; I know what foods to buy and arrangements to make for the kids. Yet familiarity doesn't make the treatment any easier. It is the hardest thing I have ever done in my life. I try to count down, telling myself that I have completed two treatments and only ten remain. After today there will be only nine. But I feel no relief, knowing that each treatment only adds to my store of accumulated memories of misery. After Marta learns that my white cell count has come back up, she administers the treatment. Dr. Moore stops by and writes my medication plan for the week. I am reminded of my children's violin teacher writing their weekly practice list— "Allegretto" by Suzuki ten times, "Minuet 2" by Bach, twelve times. Wouldn't that be a nice prescription—play beautiful music and you will get better? I leave feeling queasy, and we buy food and medication. Molly and Zach are away with friends this weekend.

I can't concentrate on movies, so I read contemporary novels about women my age. The first, to my surprise, has a character who had breast cancer and a lumpectomy followed by radiation. Then I read a mystery in which an autopsy of the woman who is murdered reveals that she had a mastectomy. The police surmise that she may have killed herself because of a recurrence. Can I never be distracted?

This weekend the nausea does not seem to abate. I call Marta on Monday, and she suggests that I continue the Zophran a bit longer. By Tuesday I'm beside myself with nausea, but I force myself to go out for dinner with David, Zach, and Molly to celebrate my birthday. I eat pasta, hoping it will calm my stomach, but I can hardly sit up. I desperately want to be in bed. I struggle to stay, to sit just a little longer so that Zach and Molly can give me their gifts. The best I can do is to be quiet, a silence that David correctly reads as a sign of my desperation. He tells me that he prefers my kicking and screaming to this. His face looks pained.

Because many people claim relief from their symptoms through acupuncture and because I'm ready to try anything, on Wednesday I call a practitioner recommended by a friend. He suggests meeting with me for two sessions to assess my situation. What could he do for my nausea? The energy flow in my body might need to be redirected, he offers. He would accomplish that through weekly meetings and massage. This is not what I had in mind. Does he use needles? I ask. He's not enthusiastic. I realize that I want needles, not regular sessions or massage. I want him to find pressure points that, when pressed, will magically result in an end to nausea. I want a quick solution, not another person diagnosing me and touching my body. I sense in his theory about my energy an accusation that I'm to blame. It's the chemo, not my misguided energy, that is at fault, I feel like screaming. I tell him I'll get back to him. Of course, I am the one who thinks that the nausea and cancer are my fault and that someone with a different personality would know how to get help from acupuncture. Why am I so resistant? Why do I deal with pain and discomfort by focusing on them every moment?

Statistics indicate that people who join cancer support groups increase their chances of surviving for five years. Yet, I'm afraid to join a group. If it included people whose diagnoses are worse than mine, I would feel undeserving of their concern and guilty about my more promising situation. On the other hand, with people whose prognoses are better than mine, people with smaller tumors who are not having chemo, I would feel envious and frightened about myself. But mainly I am afraid to hear breast cancer stories, especially those providing me with new ideas about what could go wrong. I want only a mirror image of myself, an identical twin whose prognosis is neither better nor worse than my own.

It does help to talk to friends, but even there I put up obstacles. Rather than visit with them, I choose to sleep for two hours every afternoon, to spend more time with the kids, and to go to bed early. It's not only that I feel pressed for time. I'm hiding out, keeping company with my vulnerability and nursing my wounds. I find I have little to talk about. "Yes, I'm fine," I say when friends inquire. "Not vomiting. Just a little nauseated." "What have you been doing?" I'm asked. "Not much," I reply. Just examining the nuances of my nausea, wondering if I'll die.

On Thursday I am still very sick and I call Dr. Moore. She suggests that I stop taking the Cytoxan orally; she will give me all the medications through the IV on Friday. Each treatment will take more time, but I should be less sick in the long run. She does not judge me for being nauseated, as did as my radiologist in Cambridge. It's a relief to stop taking the pills. I've grown to hate them even more as the nausea continues beyond a few days. I understand why people quit chemo. Who would "voluntarily" feel like this for six months? But I worry that, if the Cytoxan has made me this sick taken gradually for two weeks, how sick will it make me when taken all at once?

On Friday Marta explains that, before giving me the methotrexate and 5FU, she will give me saline solution and Zophran, the antinausea medication, through the IV to help me tolerate the chemotherapy. Marta talks amiably as she hangs the plastic pouches from the IV pole. After ten minutes the Zophran makes me dizzy, so Marta stops it, planning to give me the rest at the end of the treatment. She now hangs the bags containing the chemo drugs on the pole, and she starts the drip. David tries hard to keep me entertained, but we're together so much that it's hard for him to come up with new material. We joke that now we understand why so many older couples vacation with friends, not just with each other. As I watch the fluid drip from the bags through the line and into my vein, David resorts to reminiscing about the time when Zach was a baby and we took him camping across the country. It's a good try and I briefly enjoy the memories. Sometimes the drip stops, and David needs to find Marta, who comes to tap the bags and fiddle with the line. I'm vigilant about noting what I feel in my body, every flutter, every twinge, as if the chemo will keep me posted on its progress through my body. Dr. Moore comes in and writes out this weekend's medication plan. She is optimistic that this change in procedure will reduce the nausea.

That night I feel sick but must help Zach finish packing for camp the next day. I'm surprised at how quickly I am able to get him ready; we've spent so little time going over his list and shopping for the articles he needs that we must make do with what we have on hand and borrow gear from the neighbors.

Zach sits on my bed and talks with me, seeming relaxed and ready for his first extended time away from home. He insists that he is not worried about my being sick and trusts that I will be better after October. I feel very upset that he is leaving, but I keep it to myself. Separation always seems more difficult for me than for him. I promise to write often and assure him that, even though the camp does not generally allow calls home, he can ask permission of the director and call if he wants to. He says, "Oh, Mom."

After taking Zach to the bus on Saturday morning, David relates that he saw Zach sit in an empty seat where he was joined by a girl; Zach then moved quickly to a seat in the back of the bus where he could sit next to a guitar. Will he spend six hours riding to Vermont and speak to no one? We assure ourselves that he will make contact or manage on his own, as he always does. David met Laurie and Harry, who had brought their son to the bus, too. They talked about Laurie's plans for the bone marrow transplant. David gave Harry tips about medical insurance and described to him how his moods go up and down in direct proportion to mine. What a pleasant prospect for Harry. Throughout the day I am preoccupied with the thought of Laurie and how she will manage a treatment so much worse than mine.

By Thursday I feel better and am grateful for Dr. Moore's new treatment plan. My daily routine continues as usual throughout the month. I see patients from early morning until one o'clock. I read and sleep until Molly's day-camp bus drops her off downstairs at four. Surprisingly, I look forward to these naps and the time reading before I fall asleep. I'm calm during this time; my mind has been focused on work and not on illness. In the late afternoon I try, feebly, to play with Molly and I speak on the phone to friends. David picks up milk, lettuce, and fruit on the way home. He manages to serve dinner, usually courtesy of our friends. Molly and I go to bed at eight o'clock.

About nine, David comes in and sits on the bed with me. It's always the same. I cry with an intensity that does not abate from night to night. I feel more afraid in the evenings, as if my terrors, having spent the day regrouping, now wait for me in bed. To disperse them, I tell David over and over that I hate feeling sick and depressed and that I'm frightened that all this chemo will not prevent a recurrence for me. My complaints to David are so familiar that they've lost their meaning. They're like a mantra, to calm myself, or a magic formula to send my nightly demons scampering away. By the end of this ritual cleansing of my fears, we talk of brighter things—which friends we've spoken to, Molly's rendition of her day at camp, Zach's letters.

David leaves so that I can sleep and he pays bills. We've joked that, with three masters degrees and two doctorates between us, we cannot figure out our insurance coverage. He pores over explanations of services not covered and then submits the bills for these services to another insurance company. We are the lucky ones. We have three levels of coverage. All we are required to do is: Submit the bill to GHI, who will pay a percentage of what it deems a reasonable fee—that is, far less than the fee charged. Then send to Major Medical a copy of the original bill, along with GHI's explanation of services not covered. Major Medical will pay 80 percent of what it deems reasonable. Finally, send another copy of the original bill, along with explanations of services not covered by GHI or Major Medical, to our catastrophic-illness insurer, who will pay what it deems reasonable. Of the ninety-thousand-dollar likely cost of this breast cancer, we will pay only two thousand dollars. To obtain the insurance benefits, we must keep track of every bill, every check, and every explanation of benefits from each insurer, for services rendered by the anesthesiologists, radiologists, surgeons, oncologists, hospitals, and labs. This necessitates almost daily trips to a copy center for photocopies.

🔲

I decide to begin wearing my wig to work. I could get by a little longer, but I'm someone who finishes Christmas shopping by Thanksgiving and prepares the entire meal before guests arrive for dinner. I force myself to push through my anxiety and to face this humiliating first appearance in my wig. My patients seem taken aback but feign acceptance, commenting particularly on the color, which is slightly redder than my natural hair, and the style. Many of them have struggled with the idea of my hair falling out and how awful it must be to look in the mirror. One tells me that she's relieved that she need no longer come to sessions rehearsing what she'll say when she sees me with a wig. Another suggests that her hairdresser could have done a better job; he has experience with Hasidic women. I can listen to their comments with greater ease than I expected, but I'm not comfortable with this wig. It looks vaguely like human hair immediately after brushing, but it soon takes on the appearance of Dustin Hoffman's wig in *Tootsie*. I decide that I will need to return to Bits & Pieces to have it thinned.

I make an appointment and, while sitting in the chair, spot a wig that is shorter than my hair and layered. It's a style I have worn in the past and liked, so I try it on and it suits me better. I ignore the cost and buy this second one, knowing it will help me through the next six months.

Gwen writes one bill covering the cost of both, about three hundred dollars, so that I can submit it to the insurance company with my prescription from Dr. Moore for a prosthetic hair piece. If it's not covered, we'll find a way. We'll pay for this wig. We'll pay for all the cabs. We'll order take-out food for dinner. These are the hidden costs of illness that are not covered in any health plan, and we are fortunate to be able to afford them. Again I wonder how people without financial and educational resources manage this experience.

When I get home, I put the first wig away for Halloween and place the new one over the lamp in my bedroom. David points out that this will disturb the children, as it is apparently disturbing him. It's like seeing my head sitting on the dresser. Except at home I continue to wear the wig. Molly is clear, when she sees me in it, that she hates it and wants me to have my own hair back. She believes long hair is glamorous and reminds me daily that there is something wrong with how I look when I'm wearing my wig. Zach hasn't seen this wig yet, but when he saw the last one he said, "It looks good, Mom, but I'm not sure you should wear it to my school." I'm very aware of how uncomfortable it is for the kids to have their friends see me. People who don't know about my cancer think that I have a new haircut. My friends react enthusiastically. I know that their comments derive from their intuitive sense of how to ease my way. Tell me I look great; help me preserve some good feelings about my appearance, even as I feel assaulted and humiliated.

My hair continues to fall out gradually. Each morning I leave many strands on the pillow. When I wash my hair, I find a clump of it in the drain. If I run my fingers through it, I end up with a handful. Sometimes I become fascinated with the process. I distance myself from the humiliation and merely observe that my hair is falling out, as if it were happening to someone else. People volunteer tips on how to avoid losing more hair. Don't brush it; don't wash it. Why save my hair if I have to walk about with it filthy and tangled? Soak your head in a bucket of ice water after each chemo treatment. But, I reason, if the ice prevents the drugs from attacking my dividing hair cells, will it not prevent their attacking dividing cancer cells? How primitive are my formulations of how this cancer works.

Besides, I'm too fatalistic to think I could forestall this next descent into purgatory. I don't believe good behavior will keep me from losing my hair any more than I believe good thoughts will keep me from being nauseated. I have a bad attitude. I am failing at visualizing an army of chemical soldiers attacking the evil cancer cells. I'm angry but worried that my attitude makes things worse.

When my treatment for Hodgkin's disease ended, my thoughts turned toward a future of career and family. This new treatment will be followed by a decade of loss. My children will move into adolescence. David and I each have two parents who are getting older. Who will die? Our parents? Perhaps my sister, maybe me. My friend Estelle might die. Will Laurie? I have a friend who insists that the Irish dwell morbidly on death and misfortune. What choice do we have, I wonder, often coming from large, working-class families beset by illness, death, and everyday troubles? But it's not just the Irish who are busy with the dying. All of us who are now middle aged face the illness and death of our friends and relatives. I just wish I could find a way to enjoy the present despite the inevitable losses to come.

It's July 10 and the twentieth gathering of a group of friends from Harvard for an annual picnic, this year again at our house. My friends have changed the date to coincide with my break from chemo. They insist that I do no work, so I hand over control of the kitchen and spend the day catching up on people's lives. We laugh a lot, and David is very affectionate toward me, valuing, in this group of old friends, our long history.

These friendships were forged in graduate school when, despite long hours of serious academic work, we found enormous amounts of time to spend together, over coffee, over meals, in one or another of our various apartments. Our problems seemed so momentous to us then—unresponsive professors, departmental politics, tumultuous relationships, all requiring endless hours of analysis. Now, our divorces, infertility problems, illnesses, worries about aging parents barely receive a mention, so happy are we just to be together. Even my cancer takes a back seat today.

回

My chemotherapy treatment on July 16, even though it's number five, still feels like a very early stop on the long journey to the end of this ordeal. Four down still leaves eight to go. David celebrates my progress and I think he is out of his mind; to me, it seems that these treatments will never end. I set my sights on Tuesday, when I hope I can enjoy the trip with David to pick up Zach at camp. We're taking him home early so that he can have some time with me or, more honestly, so that I can have a few days with him before he and David leave on their bike trip across Iowa. Knowing how much the picnic with friends cheered me up, I hope the trip to Vermont can do the same.

Because David is out of town until late Friday, my friend Bonnie accompanies me to my appointment. Having her with me is a relief. She doesn't have the same sense of routine and accumulated dread that David and I together bring to these appointments. We talk about our work and our children. Bonnie reminds me often that her cousin who was treated for breast cancer a few years ago is doing fine.

When I am hooked up to the IV, Marta administers most of the Zophran, which again makes me feel dizzy. I feel cold from the air conditioning, so Bonnie finds a blanket. When Dr. Moore comes by, we discuss my last treatment weekend and agree that taking Ativan more regularly and sleeping through the weekend is an improvement. She asks me when I last menstruated, and I report that my last period was June 12; she is checking to see if the chemo has stopped my period. Oh, God, what if she increases my dosage because my period hasn't stopped yet?

After the treatment, I feel lightheaded and disoriented. At the deli I buy my usual strange assortment of foods—doughnuts, chicken, salad, and chocolate milk. Bonnie offers to accompany me home but I decline, knowing that David will return soon. I try to thank her for being such a good friend.

About the twelfth day of this cycle I develop a new symptom—mouth sores. Marta tells me to wash out my mouth three times a day with a solution of Maalox and Benylin to soothe the pain and fight infection. I should call her if it gets any worse. I recall seeing a woman in Dr. Moore's office who had such terrible sores on her mouth that it was hard to look at her. I feel out of control. Will I have sore gums for the rest of the treatments? Because chewing is difficult and my gums hurt, I eat selectively. Most of the sores are inside my mouth, and I hope they remain out of sight so that I can go to work without having to explain another side effect to my patients. Luckily the sores last only three days.

After a weekend of sleep I spend Monday and Tuesday working and preparing for our trip to Vermont. I find time for Molly and explain that it will be better for her to stay at her day camp than to be in the car with us for a six-hour drive to Vermont on Wednesday and then back again on Friday. I promise to bring her a gift, to call her both evenings, and to take Zach with us to pick her up at camp on Friday. Molly seems a little anxious, but she's excited about the prospect of two "sleepovers" with her friend Julia. We select two sets of shorts and tops, underwear, a book, a nightgown, and toothbrush. She also takes Lucky, the stuffed animal she gave me for Mother's Day. I have a predictably hard time sending her off on Wednesday morning. Even this simple separation tugs at me. She has had to be away from me too much. I tell myself that I'll make up for this when I have more energy.

We leave on Wednesday after I finish work. It's a beautiful day, and, although it is the week between my two chemo treatments, I feel remarkably well, even with the sick feeling in my body; perhaps it's the prospect of seeing Zach, as well as the change of scenery. Our friend Craig, the doctor, has told me that the chemicals themselves are out of my system within a few days, so what remains for weeks, the "chemo" feeling, is my body reacting to the effects of the therapy: cells dying, some of them maybe cancerous.

David and I drive for an enjoyable two hours. We talk about the kids and try to imagine Zach after a month of independence and physical activity. Our nephews and niece always returned from sleep-away camp inches taller, healthy, strong, and more mature. We've memorized Zach's letters. In the early ones he listed athletic activities but mentioned no people. I kept writing back and asking if anyone else was at camp with him. He told me to lay off. We stop for a picnic at the side of the road. David shopped at Zabar's for salads, bread, cheese, juice, and seltzer. He also brought along a lovely tablecloth, an unprecedented act that I recognize as an expression of love. For twenty years he has been oblivious to the nuances of a meal, the ceremony of eating. I am not. He did this just for me and it gives me untold pleasure.

We drive on and stop for a lovely visit with one of David's former professors and his wife, who spend summers in Vermont. When I was recovering from Hodgkin's disease, they arranged jobs for us as caretakers of a summer camp now used by the Marlboro Music Festival. In exchange for rolling the tennis courts and closing the gates, we had the run of an old house with a big porch overlooking a pristine lake and surrounded by pine trees.

It was in Vermont that I discovered my hearing loss. I answered the phone and could hear nothing, although I learned later that my friend could hear me so the connection was fine. I went to a specialist in Brattleboro who told me that I had no hearing in my left ear and that there was no way to tell if it would return. "You have another ear," he said. Perhaps the loss was caused by a virus, perhaps by the radiation. I remember the radiology supervisor at Peter Bent Brigham correcting the technicians who had aimed the radiation too high, near my ear. They then aimed it lower, perhaps too near my breast. Perhaps the radiation that saved my life took my hearing and my breast. Perhaps not.

David and I talk about a second summer we spent at that lake in Vermont. I was pregnant with Zach and desperate to hold on to him after my miscarriage the previous January. We rowed in a boat on the lake and talked about names for him. I was nauseated, but for a happy reason. I vomited into the lake.

Later we drive to the inn where we have reserved a room. We are the only guests of the innkeeper, an eccentric British woman who walks me through her perennial garden and sends us off to dinner down the road. The restaurant serves salad from the owner's meticulously kept vegetable garden and a wonderful meal. Much is happening among our fellow diners. A professor from Dartmouth ignores a greeting from someone who has just read his latest book. Two men in their fifties enter the dining room with well-dressed young women on their arms. The members of a large and seemingly dysfunctional family argue their way through dinner. A veritable Peyton Place. We can hardly wait to see Zach tomorrow, so after dinner we drive in the dark to get a look at his camp. David regales me with the same boyhood camp stories I've heard a hundred times. I love all that is familiar about this day together.

After a greasy, thoroughly English breakfast the next morning, I call Marta to check on the time of my chemo appointment Friday. She tells me that I am not scheduled to have chemo this week; the switch to IV treatments means that I am now on a three-week schedule with only one treatment per cycle. This is not my understanding. She will check when Dr. Moore, now on vacation, calls in. I'm upset by this disruption of my expectations but assume that after Marta speaks to Dr. Moore she will schedule me for a Friday appointment.

We visit with the innkeeper, who's delighted that we've heard of the philosopher and theologian Emanuel Swedenborg; in this small Vermont town she meets weekly with a group of Swedenborgians to discuss his writings. When I tell her about my breast cancer, she pronounces that her mother cured herself of cancer by eating carrots.

We spend the morning in Hanover, New Hampshire, and visit the Dartmouth College library. We call the camp and arrange to pick Zach up at three o'clock. We arrive early, sit in Adirondack chairs, and watch some teenaged boys play tennis while some teenaged girls pretend to ignore them. The posted schedule indicates that Zach is swimming, but a counselor suggests that he may be in his cabin. We knock on the door and he opens it. He looks beautiful—tan, tall, strong, and rested. It's awkward for him; we look different, I in my new wig and David with shorter hair. He silently struggles to adjust to us in the presence of friends. He hugs me awkwardly. I remember when he was six and I returned ahead of David from a ten-day trip to Hungary. Zach got off the bus from camp and fell into my arms sobbing, telling me that it was hard having me away, that he was used to Daddy taking trips but not me. God, I never want to go away from him. I never want to die and leave him.

As he gives us the tour of camp, other kids greet him matter-of-factly. He has his own world here, a world he obviously loves. He shows us the lake, the dining hall, the basketball hoops, and the archery equipment; gradually he becomes more comfortable with us. After we gather his belongings, he says a nonchalant goodbye to his friends and tolerates some gushing and hugs from his counselors. Zach talks nonstop during the four-hour drive to our weekend house, where we'll spend the night. We visit a gift shop where he buys a souvenir for Molly, nothing for himself. I love the ride with him, these precious hours filled with "philosophical" thoughts, as his counselors must have called them, delivered with boyish ardor. If I could just stay alive until he grows up, just not interrupt this natural unfolding.

We take him out for dinner and he orders politely. He jokes about my ordering red meat, acknowledging his memory of how I deal with chemo. I ask him if it was hard to get used to me in my wig. Relieved that I have asked he says, "Yeah, I almost didn't recognize you. And Dad looked weird, too." At the house he sits on the couch and reads us every letter we wrote to him at camp, letting us know by this reading how much our connection to him meant, how much he loved the letters.

In the morning I drink coffee on the porch and begin to feel afraid. Marta is still waiting to learn from Dr. Moore whether I should have chemo today. What if I were on a three-week schedule? It would mean fewer treatments and that would be a relief. But to my surprise I find myself wanting the four-week schedule, believing that more is better. It strikes me that, in my own whiney way, I am fighting for my life.

What if Dr. Moore's call to Marta is too late for treatment today and I have to wait for the treatment until Monday? Because David and Zach are leaving for their bike trip together in Iowa tomorrow, I have carefully planned the week. Molly will stay with David's parents for the weekend, while I recover. Then friends will help me manage during the week. If my treatment is delayed, I will be sick on Tuesday and Wednesday, when I planned to work and be with Molly. The prospect terrifies me. I haven't functioned much as a parent in the past three months, let alone as a nauseated parent by myself. And how will David enjoy himself if he knows I am struggling to work and take care of Molly when I'm so sick?

We pick up Molly on our drive home. Although Zach's behavior toward her is cool, he is obviously happy to see her. Molly adores him. I learn from Marta that, in fact, I was due for a treatment today. Now it's too late. She is apologetic and asks if I can come on Monday instead. I'm angry.

I hang up and fall apart. What if I can't do it? I've never worked the day after a treatment. I cannot cancel my appointments with patients. I cannot admit that I'm too sick. I cannot give up the fragile hold I have on my normal life. I'm sobbing again. When I had Hodgkin's disease, the doctor reduced the amount of radiation I was given in each treatment because I was vomiting so much. He failed to explain that this meant extending my four-week cycle to six weeks. I had to cancel a visit to my family in Buffalo. I was devastated. So much was already out of my control that the delay felt catastrophic, as does this.

Molly and Zach work hard at consoling me. Zach says, "Don't worry, Mom. We'll figure it out." Molly simply puts her arms around me and hugs me. Although I love their nurturing, it signals to me that I, not they, better act like a parent. I take a deep breath and tell them, "I'm all right now. Let's make a plan." To everyone's relief I take charge, arranging for David's parents to pick Molly up on Sunday evening, keep her at their home on Monday, and drive her to camp Tuesday morning. She will take the bus to our apartment on Tuesday afternoon. I feel calmer in having a plan but still shaky about the week. The degree of my fragility and my lack of resilience astound me.

It's very difficult for David to leave. Although far from noble, I now try to communicate clearly that I want him to go with Zach, that the trip will be good for both of them. David has taken on my burdens so generously. Why have I made him feel as if he's abandoning me? We both know that my breakdown after hearing from Marta grew out of my fears about coping this week without him. I emphasize to him that I can rearrange a few of my Monday appointments; Dinitia will go with me on Monday for the treatment. Betsy will bring me steak and soup for dinner on Wednesday; Keir will put Molly on the bus each morning. I will sleep in the afternoon until four o'clock when she returns.

David will try to call from Iowa, but he knows that ten thousand cyclists will be competing for phones in the small Iowa towns where they stop. He and Zach will bike 585 miles. Zach is in good physical shape; David is not. His plans to train for the trip have been curtailed by my illness. Still, he and Zach have managed some good practice rides. I feel a little envious. I purchased the first good bike in the family so that I would have an activity to share with Zach as he got older. Now it's their activity. I try to believe that next summer I will feel strong enough to cycle with them.

David and Zach leave early on Saturday, packed according to David's method of throwing a few things in a bag. I surmise that they will find themselves without underwear, but I'm learning that I cannot control everything, or much of anything for that matter. They promise to drop us a note soon. I plan to write this evening so that David will receive my letter by our anniversary on Wednesday.

Molly and I have a lovely day, in spite of the weekend's botched plans. We walk in the park and go to a movie. We visit a bookstore, where we run into my friend Arlene, who is distraught because her partner, Estelle, who also is my friend, has been diagnosed with a cancer in her lungs and bones. Arlene is clearly terrified and desperate to do something. She is in the middle of a nightmare that already sounds worse than mine.

In the children's book section, Molly spots a hardcover copy of *The Secret Garden,* packaged with a small gold key on a gold chain. I am tired and sense that this is the beginning of the end. We already have *The Secret Garden* and sometime I will find her a similar necklace, but not now, I tell her. She is furious and cries all the way out of the bookstore. I take her to Burger King as promised, and she sits across from me, scowling as she eats French fries and refuses to talk. Outside, she begins to beg for the book again, and I scream at her to cut it out. She cries but gets the point. At home I finally manage to pull myself together and calm her down. We spend a nice evening together. We crawl into my bed and we each write letters to David and Zach; then I read to her. She reminds me of *The Secret Garden* book but does so without the histrionics.

On Sunday I read the *New York Times* while Molly plays with a friend. In the evening Sophie and Alex come to pick Molly up, and we have dinner out before they leave. When we return to their car, we discover that the bag of Molly's clothes that we had placed in the trunk has been stolen. Molly is very upset, and we each try to console her with tales of having been robbed ourselves. How bizarre that we think our stories will minimize her distress over her stolen possessions. So like those cancer stories that people tell me. I spend the evening composing a book of crossword puzzles for Molly because her favorite one was stolen with her clothes. I want to make up for her loss.

Monday morning I see patients until it is time to meet Dinitia to go for my treatment. We arrive to find the waiting room filled with people who look very sick, sicker than

I have ever seen people here. Most disturbing is a young man who is obviously dying. He sits with his wife and young son. People in wheelchairs arrive and leave after their chemo.

During my treatment Dinitia distracts me with the details of her interview with a celebrity she is writing about for *New York Magazine*. We talk about her summer plans to teach at the Breadloaf Writers' Conference. If she's rattled by seeing me receive chemotherapy, she's doing a great job of disguising it. I am touched by her offers of help this week. A young, male doctor who is substituting for Dr. Moore reviews my medication schedule and writes the necessary prescriptions for Zophran and Ativan. Sometimes I'm struck by how ludicrous these names are, and I picture a committee of advertising executives at some drug company thinking them up. How about Nausinex or Vomitrim? I miss Dr. Moore and smile at myself when I think of how strongly attached I am to this woman I hardly know. I've come to depend on her to guide me through this dangerous territory.

Tuesday I see patients, surprised that I am managing so well on the first day after a treatment, pacing myself so that I can get through to nap time. I sleep until Molly returns at four o'clock. When David calls on Wednesday, I can report that we are managing well. In fact, I feel a bit euphoric about our successful week together. David tells me that he received the "love letter" I sent to commemorate our anniversary. He is clearly touched by reading about what I feel but do not say often enough to him: how deeply grateful I am for his love and constancy; how I could not endure this without him; how I sometimes look at him and know how terrified he is of the possibility that he will lose me, and how it breaks my heart; how I know that Molly and Zach will survive this because he is always such a loving parent.

On Thursday I take Molly to see our pediatrician because she has what looks like poison ivy near her eye. He had suggested that I watch her eye for a few more days, but because I feel so vulnerable I prefer that he look at her. He examines her eye and concludes that she has some kind of allergic reaction that should clear up on its own. He talks with me for an hour, concerned about my breast cancer and upset himself because his wife recently left him for another man. This affair completely shocked his orthodox Jewish community, he tells me. He worries about having enough time for his three children, who continue to live with him, and he struggles to understand his part in the failure of his marriage. This man has taken care of my children since Molly was born, and I have always valued his generosity. But this is the first time we have talked so intimately. The conversation is like a gift that I carry with me the rest of the day.

Molly and I find this weekend in the city less satisfying, perhaps because the beautiful weather makes us miss the country. David and Zach return on Sunday, excited and brimming with stories. I'm so glad to have them home, and I want to enjoy them and their adventures. But soon I'm crying again, as if all the feelings I managed to suppress can no longer be controlled. The week was apparently harder for me than I thought, and I regret that David comes home to find me in this state. Why can't I show him how well I've done? Why must I always be like a needy child with him? Am I punishing him for going away?

At the end of my July cycle David and I join friends to celebrate Jerry's birthday. I have just spoken to Jan, who had a breast reduction along with her mastectomy. She tells me that her doctor, having approved the surgery for her, now says that the scar tissue interferes with his ability to examine her breasts for lumps. I listen but ignore the implications for her; I think only of myself and am off and running with my fears of a recurrence that I now imagine will remain undiscovered if I have breast reduction. I call up all the terror-inducing comments of Dr. Klauber: If the cancerous process was taking place in my left breast, why not in my right? Even if a biopsy of the right breast shows nothing, cancer could still be lurking secretly in its other tissues. I become obsessed again with the idea of a second mastectomy. I try to assure myself that, if a new cancer developed in my other breast, we would probably catch it early and I could have CMF again. But the thought of more chemo is too horrible; better to get rid of this breast now, to make this decision while this unbearable treatment is fresh in my mind. I unsettle my friends with these bizarre thoughts—as if it is normal to go to a birthday party and talk about breasts, cutting off breasts, and never forgetting that they pose a mortal danger to one's well being.

Chapter seven

Despair

It is August 4 and I am scheduled for a liver scan, which, like the bone scan I will have next week, will provide Dr. Moore with an outline of my insides. I have thought little about these scans, assuming they are being done to establish a base-line with which future scans can be compared. Today it occurs to me that they can also be used to check for tumors and I become worried. David meets me at the radiology lab, still under construction, on East Seventy-second Street. An elevator takes us from the cavernous lobby to the basement, where the offices are located. I check in with the receptionist and wait. Many of the people waiting are being diagnosed and are very worried. We overhear an older woman discussing her bill at the desk. The clerk knows that the woman is covered by Medicare but she must pay five hundred dollars today. The woman says she's sorry, but she doesn't have the money with her right now. I admire the grace with which she delivers this understatement.

On Friday, between sessions with patients, I find a message on my answering machine to call the secretary at the lab where I had my liver scan. When I call, he tells me that they found something suspicious on my scan and that I will need a sonogram. Without registering my hysteria, I schedule the sonogram for next Wednesday, immediately before the bone scan. In the one minute I have before my next patient arrives, I phone David at his office. Can he call Dr. Moore to get more information while I'm in my next session? He is furious that I received this information by phone from a stranger and, though trying to reassure me, he's worried.

I greet my next patient and struggle unsuccessfully to put aside my fear and concentrate on her. Rarely am I this distracted in a session but I'm terrified that the cancer has spread to my liver and that I am going to die. I try to take hold of the possibility David suggested—that the scan has picked up something insignificant that requires further tests. Luckily, my patient is talkative and I have time to compose myself. Only by an act of incredible will do I manage to focus my attention on her. As soon as she leaves, I listen to a message from David telling me that Dr. Moore is not worried about the liver scan. The doctor at the lab had called her and described what seems to be an irregularity in the shape of my liver. She told him not to call me, that she would discuss it with me on Friday; she is annoyed about this unnecessary scare. Obviously the exigencies of the lab schedule prevailed.

I return the next Wednesday for a liver sonogram and a bone scan. I am now much more anxious because of the scare, and I struggle to believe that my irregularly shaped liver is of no significance. But I know that there must be other possibilities; why else would they follow up with more tests? Now attuned to the huge potential for irregularities, I imagine the multitude of odd shapes that my skeleton could take.

Although quite straightforward, the liver sonogram takes a long time. I lie on my back on a table in a dimly lit room. The technician runs a hand-held instrument over my stomach and presses it on my right side where my liver resides. She watches a screen that shows my liver, and she is far too engrossed to talk with me. This leaves me ample time to think. After twenty minutes she leaves the room, saying that she will show the pictures to the doctor and be back shortly. When she returns, she tells me that she needs to get a clearer picture. "To get a clearer picture," the familiar, dreaded words I heard after my mammogram. She moves the instrument about as if looking for something. I lie silently, too terrified to speak, yet knowing that speech is my only chance for reassurance if there is any to be had. I tell her that the need to get a clearer picture worries me and she assures me that it does not mean that there's a problem; sometimes it's just hard to get a good look. She goes out again and comes back to tell me that I can leave now.

I return to the waiting room and am soon called by the technician who will do the bone scan. She is an attractive woman, petite, with pretty dark eyes, short curly hair, and an energetic yet professional demeanor. She explains that she will inject into a vein in my arm a dye that contains a low level of radioactive particles. Then I can leave for two hours while the dye circulates throughout my body. When I return, she will do the tests. For the bone scan I will lie flat on a table, which will slide slowly back and forth so that the machine overhead can take pictures of my entire skeleton. Essentially, the machine will record the number of radioactive particles in my body; the particles will show up more strongly where there is activity in the bone—indicating cancer, arthritis, a fracture, or an infection. In other words, I think, there's a good possibility that a problem will be picked up, and nothing at this point would indicate whether it's arthritis or cancer, whether I should be terrified or not. There'll be no discomfort, and she'll play some classical music to help make the time pass quickly. She injects the dye and sends me off to lunch.

David and I discuss where to eat. We have frequented, or contaminated, two restaurants in this neighborhood already. In the early weeks of my breast cancer, when I was often quite shaken, we went to a comfortable Italian restaurant with red checkered tablecloths and good bread. We sat and tried to absorb information from the early visits to Dr. Cody. David talked about his relief that I had had a mammogram and the lump had been found so early; I felt no relief and only imagined the treatment. My attempts to envision a time when I might go to a restaurant and feel normal failed. I only imagined feeling profound separateness and sadness forever.

Today we choose the other restaurant, Cafe Greco, because it has a lunch special. It is a large restaurant on three levels, each filled with small tables with white tablecloths and lovely bouquets of flowers. Seated at the surrounding tables are older women, some whose hair has a blue cast, some whose face lifts and coiffured hair, instead of hiding their age, make them look as if they're wearing masks of their younger selves. I admire their liveliness as they lunch with friends. I am envious of them even in their advanced age, ignoring that the possibility of impending death must often cross their minds, too.

When we return for the scan, we notice a young woman in her midtwenties being consoled by her boyfriend. It is apparent that she has just heard some bad news. They remind us of our selves and the pain we endured in hearing my first diagnosis. They seem too young to deal with a medical crisis. How will they preserve their relationship? We barely managed. We joke now that cancer kept us together, that were it not for guilt David would have left. But it took years for our relationship to recover. And how will they pay the bills? My insurance did not cover all my medical bills for Hodgkin's disease. Because neither I nor my parents had the money to pay even the small amount I owed, I simply ignored the bills. One day during my radiation treatments, David answered a call from a collection agent and began screaming, "Don't you understand, this woman is sitting here with cancer? How can you harass her with bills?" The calls stopped, and eventually the hospital wrote off the balance. But a few years later when I saw a specialist for my hearing loss, I had to pay up front to be seen. What happens now to people who cannot pay?

I also notice an older woman in her seventies whose daughter has brought her for tests. It's clear that they are trying to get through an immediate crisis, as if it's temporary. That's how I managed with Hodgkin's disease and how I manage now; and it's how I imagine people cope even at the age of ninety—by viewing each health crisis as a temporary one. At the moment I know better; I know that my future holds frequent tests, anxious intervals waiting for results, and unimagined medical problems. This is the case for everyone, David comments; sooner or later something goes wrong with these bodies of ours. But I seem to have a jump on a lot of people, I point out.

The technician finally calls me for the bone scan. My bladder must be empty for the test, so I run to the bathroom and then put on the robe she gave me, still not sure if it should be open in the back or front. I reenter the room and am asked to lie still on the table and not move my head. Having my skeleton copied is an eerie experience, like auditioning for Halloween, or for death. The scanning process is slow and, although the technician is in the room, I feel as if I'm alone. I try to imagine what Molly and Zach are doing now and to ignore the anomalies the machine overhead may be registering.

Lying under this machine reminds me of my radiation treatments for Hodgkin's disease. As I lay on that table in Boston, I was watched on a TV screen not only by the technicians outside the room, but also by the doctors, nurses, and even patients who happened to walk by. I never really understood why they had to watch me on a monitor. Were they afraid I would run away?

My mind drifts to the discussion David and I had over lunch. He's skeptical about the extensive use of certain medical tests. They're often unnecessary, he argued, but are prescribed to help cover the costs of expensive machinery. I pointed out that this radiology lab is not part of a small hospital struggling to pay for its own machine; it's a centralized center to which many doctors at many hospitals refer patients, so there's less incentive for unnecessary tests. He moved on to the next potential problem. The nature of certain tests is that they turn up anomalies that, though not medical problems, require further testing. If an anomaly is found, the doctor must prescribe further tests to rule out disease. Great. The bone scan might turn up an anomaly and I'll need even more tests to rule out cancer. Or it might turn up a real problem, as my mammogram did. In what individual cases do you choose not to follow up?

I begin to think of the concerns that arise simply because you are someone who must be watched closely by a doctor. Not only do you enter a system that sometimes has a life of its own, you also become the victim of zealous doctors. A few years ago I had an internist who, because of my history, kept finding problems where there were none. I had a cyst on my back that needed to be lanced. Alarmed that it might be a sign of something more serious, he arranged to have a dermatologist see me that day. I spent hours in panicky isolation, baffled about what kind of cancer exhibits itself as an oozing cyst. Gina, who was living in New York then, picked up the kids after school while

David met me at the doctor's office. It was, in fact, a cyst that needed to be lanced. Some months later, before leaving with the kids for Disney World, I went to see this doctor again because I had a terrible cold that had settled in my chest. He thought my lungs sounded fine, but while examining me he felt a lump on my neck. He looked grim as he took blood for tests whose results would not be available until the next Tuesday. Another vacation ruined by anxiety, I thought; but on the plane that night, after a day of terror and endless fingering of my neck, I discovered a matching lump on the other side of my neck. Recalling David's "lump," I concluded that what the doctor discovered was probably just part of my anatomy and not cancer. I calmed down considerably, trying to enjoy Disney World with the kids, until Tuesday, when I learned that everything was normal. It was time for a new doctor.

My thoughts return to the morbid mapping of my insides. I try not to picture my skeleton, myself as a skeleton. Finally, it's over; I leave the building with giant sobs welling up inside me. What's wrong with me? It was just a test. I tell David how frightened I am that the cancer has already spread to a different place in my body. He reminds me that none of my lymph nodes were cancerous and that it's not logical to think that the cancer will be found elsewhere. As if anything about this is logical, I think.

As I approach my August chemo, I realize that, unlike the May and June cycles, I found very little relief from the feeling of sickness after my chemo treatments in July. I have been trying in vain to note my progress with each succeeding treatment and to envision the end. In college I got through exam week by imagining vacations to follow. When I have the flu, I anticipate feeling better in a few days. But these tricks fail me now. Having undergone two-thirds of the prescribed chemotherapy, I feel no relief. When I wake in the middle of the night before a treatment, I sit for a while and look out my bedroom window; all the lights are out in the apartment building across the street. This is the time when I think my unmentionable thoughts—that if I die I want my children to move on with their lives, yet I feel sad at the thought that they will think of me only once in a while, in the form of whatever memories they have of me; that sometimes I understand what my friend who has cancer meant last week when she told me about puking in the toilet while her husband held her hair back: she wanted to say to him that she couldn't go on with this chemo anymore, but she knew that this was the one thing he could not hear.

When I speak to Dr. Moore, she informs me, to my relief, that my bone scan and liver sonogram are normal. I tell her how tormented I continue to be by the question of a second mastectomy, particularly as I try to decide whether to have my other breast reduced. I reason that it would be efficient to simply have another mastectomy at the time of my second implant surgery in December but that I need to decide soon. She suggests that, rather than decide now, I proceed with the reduction of my right breast in December. The reduction will yield a good sample of tissue to examine; if it's clean, I might feel safer about not having a mastectomy; if there's a problem, I can proceed accordingly. She calms me, as always, by being utterly reasonable and offering me a way out of my rigid conceptualization of a problem. I have wanted to share responsibility for this decision, and she lets me.

After my second chemo in August, I begin a two-week vacation in the country. Although I expect to be sick for a few days, I in fact feel good enough to be out of bed. I spend time sitting on the deck, reading and talking with the kids. I am almost ecstatic at the thought that life might feel normal again, sometime. I even cook. People stop by. I'd like to forego wearing my wig, but there are many kids coming and going and I don't want to embarrass Zach and Molly. Lately it's been harder on them, as David gently pointed out, to see me without my wig, because I've lost most of my hair. I've left the remaining strands long. They look ridiculous and I should probably cut them, but I don't, perhaps as a pathetic last stand against complete baldness.

This first Sunday of my vacation I open the *New York Times* to find on the front cover of the magazine section a photographic self-portrait taken after her mastectomy by the artist and political activist Matuschka. She is covered by a thin veil and looks anorectic and deathlike. Although I know she is making a statement, I cannot get beyond my feeling of shock to decipher the meaning of this photograph. Why must she depict this mastectomy as so horrific? Is this the only way to communicate the havoc that breast cancer wreaks on women's bodies? I think of photos I've recently seen of women after their mastectomies. I found them comforting in their ordinariness; they are still the same women, not apparitions of their former selves.

David points out that my critical judgment seems to be at an all-time low; art is not supposed to simply record life but to comment on it. "It's easy for you to say," I respond. " All your friends are not thinking of you as they gaze at this photo over their morning coffee."

We need soil to fill in the area surrounding the deck we built last year. We can purchase two yards for one hundred dollars or ten yards for two hundred dollars. I know that I cannot shovel much now, but I order the larger quantity anyway, thinking of it as an investment in a future time when I will be strong again. David forgoes his usual resistance to a project and agrees enthusiastically, encouraged by the prospect of my eventually returning to my former self.

I do find the energy to make a shade bed for plants near the deck. Zach, who generally procrastinates with chores, works surprisingly hard with me. Because I am trying to be careful with my left arm to prevent it from filling up with fluid, as can happen after the removal of lymph nodes, he shovels and carries the soil and peat moss. He is solicitous of me, perhaps sensing how fragile I feel and knowing what a good sign it is that I'm active at all. We plant the hostas given me by a friend and we transplant some native ferns from the brook. As inexperienced gardeners, we have no idea whether the transplantation will work, but we proceed eagerly. Zach carefully cradles the ferns he has dug up, places them in their holes, and, becoming more confident, transplants some day lilies. I cover the bed with pine mulch and he edges it with rocks he has gathered from the woods. We both feel exhilarated and proud of our efforts, and we luxuriate in David and Molly's praise.

We have ordered tickets to a Beach Boys concert at the Saratoga Center for the Performing Arts, knowing that the kids will recognize the songs from listening to tapes in the car. I'm not feeling great and am worried that this attempt at normalcy will backfire. As we drive to Saratoga, I look forward to a good meal but adjust my expectations to Pizza Hut. Before the concert we walk about the grounds filled with people buying food at refreshment stands or playing Frisbee on the lawn. Other people stroll arm in arm, and I feel a pang of longing for the kind of easy way they share their bodies. I feel so battered. At best, I ignore my body, which isn't hard, given that I live so much in my mind lately, trying to keep my rampaging thoughts under control. I am in my separate world tonight, desolate again, with sickness as my closest companion, offering me only negativity. I take Molly to the ladies' room, where she washes up and masters the hand-drying machines. In the mirror I catch a glimpse of myself in my wig, looking worn and tired. Cancer comes with me even on vacation.

As we move toward the auditorium, I realize that I cannot sit for hours without drinking fluids, so I get a cup of water. When we give our tickets to the usher at the entrance, she tells me that drinks are not allowed. I politely explain that I am sick and need to drink a lot of water. She looks me directly in the eye and says, "If you're sick, why didn't you stay home in bed?"

I feel myself crumble and leave the auditorium. David puts his arm around me, knowing that I am close to falling apart. He is furious at this woman's coldness, and the children are upset, too. Molly hugs me and says, "Don't cry, Mommy," and Zach takes up my cause: "She shouldn't tell sick people they can't come in." Finally I compose myself to go back in, without the water. I look past the usher as we head for our seats. David stops to speak to her, while the other ushers listen. He explains, quite angrily, that I am undergoing chemotherapy for cancer and that, although I need water, I don't need to be in bed. She should think more carefully about what she says to people. I'm surprised by this uncharacteristically aggressive action of his and by his satisfaction with it. I sit, tired and thirsty, but comforted and protected by the righteous indignation of my little family.

The Beach Boys enter the stage, looking like Miami Beach retirees. Perhaps afraid that they can no longer hold an audience by themselves, they surround themselves with young female dancers dressed in scant bikinis. Usually I would find this spectacle simply ludicrous, but tonight I find it offensive. These women are showing off their legs and breasts in order to titillate an audience that might otherwise feel ripped off. Am I voicing a good feminist critique or simply being prudish? Perhaps I'm just envious. The glorification of these ideal, young female bodies makes my loss of a breast that much harder to bear.

It is the first week of September, and I return from vacation to resume work and start cycle five of chemotherapy. I feel depressed and discouraged that I'm not done with these treatments, jolted back from the more normal life I had on vacation. I'm glad to see my patients again, and I learn that a number of them reacted more strongly to my cancer during this vacation than they had earlier, perhaps because my absence made their fear of losing me more palpable. My work with them brings me right back to the heart of the matter: they would miss me if I died.

The chemo treatment goes along as usual. This time I speak to a few women in the waiting room; one woman, who has come for a follow-up appointment with Dr. Moore, looks great and generously offers me encouragement. I cannot believe that I will ever feel or look well again. Another woman, who is a little older than I but at an earlier point in her chemo, talks about her anxieties about gaining weight and losing her hair. I commiserate with her while David watches. He later teases me about how self-assured I appear to others; he, of course, knows otherwise. He comes home every day to find me depressed, sick, worn down, angry. Before now David had never experienced real depression. He does now. He tells me how hard it is to get out of bed, how sometimes nothing seems to have meaning, how trapped in misery he feels. I know that, like me, he is finding it harder to envision a different life, our normal life. In fact, this has come to feel like normal life, and we strain to hold on to some sense that it will ever be different. Although I am familiar with the routine of chemotherapy treatments, the experience has become no easier, because the nausea no longer diminishes a few days after treatment. I never actually vomit, so it's hard for me to accept that I feel this miserable, just from nausea. But the sick feeling continues throughout the month, and my emotional reserves are completely depleted.

I tell Dr. Moore that I'm tired of hearing about breast cancer as a chronic disease. I understand that this formulation encourages patients to pay attention to their diets, to be responsible about checkups, and to take good care of themselves. But I may very well be free of breast cancer. And, if I'm not, what good does viewing myself as having a chronic disease do? Why should I tell myself that I will have this disease forever? She's sympathetic and assures me that my Hodgkin's disease was an acute episode, as is this breast cancer. The treatments will end, and I will return to ordinary life. I know she has given me another of those gifts, a new way of conceptualizing this illness. There are no guarantees that this cancer will not recur, but this episode will probably be the end of it, and she gives me permission to leave it behind me if I can.

During September the nausea is worse than ever. Each day merges into the next in a kind of grayness. Because of an asbestos crisis the opening of the public schools is delayed for two weeks. Yet even this unscheduled complication seems of little consequence. The events of daily life take on no particular shape. Somehow I do what must be done. I arrange for ballet, violin, and piano lessons, for play dates to fill up the two weeks. Most of the burden falls on David, who cannot handle much more. He becomes quieter as I become needier. I am worn out beyond belief.

It remains uncannily true, however, that I pull myself together to see patients. Although my wig is always a reminder of my chemotherapy, some of my patients never mention the chemo, some always begin by asking how I am doing, some are surprised to realize that they've stopped thinking about it very much. My stance with my patients is that I'm managing well, which seems to be true when I'm working. I'm basically the same person I was before and I work with them in the same way.

More and more each patient's idiosyncratic reactions to my breast cancer unfold. One woman feels that, now that I've had surgery, I can understand the feeling she lives with all the time, though for no physical reason—that her body is damaged, that there is something wrong with her. Patients who have had surgery themselves recall in detail its effect on their lives, including their helplessness and vulnerability. One woman is preoccupied with the fear that, if I die, no one will inform her of my death. A number have dreams about their hair falling out. One man struggles with his discomfort in knowing something so personal about me; another wishes that he could protect me and has trouble depending on me. When any of my patients hear of someone dying of breast cancer their fears about me return.

Still, I realize that it's hard for my patients to talk about themselves, knowing my situation, and I sometimes wonder if it's fair to them that I continue to work. Although they talk to me about their interactions with me and with the people in their lives, and about their dreams, my illness is always in the background, a threat to the continuation of their relationship with me. I worry that I sometimes insist too vigorously that they believe I will be fine. Perhaps their worries, on top of mine and my family's, are at times too much to bear.

On Tuesday, September 14, I see Dr. Breckman for my final weekly appointment to inflate the expander. Just as Dr. Cody predicted, the expander has a kind of bionic appearance and protrudes directly outward from my body. Dr. Breckman notices that it has expanded more on the side under my arm than is desirable. I appreciate his articulating this peculiarity. Something had looked awry, but I couldn't determine what was wrong. He will try to make an adjustment in surgery.

We review the plans for my December surgery. Because it will have been eight months since my last surgery, I will need to have an electrocardiogram and blood tests again, but not a chest x-ray. In addition to having him insert the permanent implant, I have finally decided to have him do a breast reduction on the right side, ostensibly to get a good sample of tissue to be examined at the lab but perhaps to have matching breasts. He asks me again about the size of the permanent implant I want. I try, as often before, to engage him in a discussion about how large these breasts will end up being, but with no better success.

I leave his office having no scheduled appointment for a few months, and I'm struck by the fact that in thirteen appointments he's never asked me how I am doing, no matter how green I appear or how crooked my wig is. I must remember that this is a doctor who chose a specialty in which people would not be sick and die. He doesn't want to know.

I plan a weekend away with David and the kids so that we'll have something to look forward to after my two September treatments. I reserve a room in a motel near Sag Harbor on Long Island for the weekend of September 24.

The September cycle seems endless. I feel terrible most of the time; my system must be either saturated with noxious chemicals or so worn down that each treatment is harder to take. I drink more water than ever and switch from butterscotch to peppermint Lifesavers. I'm probably due for some time with my dentist, but I can't deal with that now. Lifesavers aren't great for the teeth, and my gums have been too sore to floss. I cry even more frequently than before. People try in vain to cheer me with the thought that chemotherapy will soon be over.

Our daily routine has become truly horrible. Each afternoon I make a useless vow to be better natured. When Molly and Zach return from school, I manage to prepare a snack and inquire about their day; but, at the first sign of bickering, complaining, or nagging, I scream at them. When David is at home, I make myself scarce to protect the children from my wrath; but then I think of my patients whose depressed mothers stayed in their rooms, leaving their children feeling abandoned and angry, and I worry. Although I am conscious of how much I love David, I communicate nothing but rage. I greet him with my litany of complaints; I show no interest in his day; I am angry at him for everything. He does the shopping, but the bananas are too big, not ripe, too ripe. He bought too much lettuce and not enough milk; he forgot to call his parents. David is afraid to speak for fear of saying something that will set me off. I feel abandoned, and then I am furious at him for withdrawing.

He begins to fight back and to argue with me. At one level, I'm glad that he's not allowing me to demolish him, but I'm also hurt—underneath my rage is my desperate need for him, fueled now by his anger and withdrawal. I feel myself unraveling completely. The children are caught up in our nightmare. We snap at them. They snap at us and at each other. We have no patience. We spend little time with them except to issue orders. Zach slams his door. Molly stomps off in a huff and throws herself on the bed crying. We are a family out of control.

I search for books written by women with breast cancer, but I find few descriptions that fit my experience. I resent reading glib, cute stories about cancer not being so bad, and I hate hearing that cancer has made someone a better person. It's only making me a worse person.

My friend Estelle continues to undergo elaborate tests to determine the source of the very aggressive cancer in her chest and bones. Her doctors have begun chemo, using drugs targeted for either breast or lung cancer. The prognosis does not sound good. Yet, when we talk, she generously expresses interest in me. Each time we converse, I realize that a cancer that has metastasized could be my fate too. On the nights after we talk, I'm in turmoil. No matter how calm I may be while talking to Estelle, my sleep is filled with nightmares about dying.

The same is true for me with Laurie as she undergoes a bone marrow transplant and teeters again and again on the brink of death. I am part of the circle of friends who stand watchfully at her bedside, some literally and others, like me, only figuratively. I hear about the infections, the weakness, and the delirium. I feel too fragile to see Laurie or Estelle in a gaunt, bald, and weak state, to see in them my own worst fears, so I do not visit them in the hospital. I feel like a coward for avoiding them in the way some people avoided me. Yet I so readily identify with them that I would be overwhelmed if I saw them, and I need to protect myself in order to finish these treatments.

On the second Friday with no chemo appointment, David and I visit a public school that we are considering for Zach for grades seven and eight. We have to make a decision soon, but the task of looking at middle schools and sorting out our options seems monumental. We can worry but we cannot act. Clearly, our anxiety about schools is disproportionate to the situation. We are not rational parents trying to make a wise decision, but two traumatized parents who consider the world a very dangerous place from which our children need to be protected. We want a school that will take care of everything we cannot handle: one that will motivate Zach to do his homework and love math, science, and literature; that will keep him engaged after school in music and sports; that will shelter and protect him from the world. Although we are strong believers in public school, we discuss private school as well, desperate to find some place that will take over for us. And this school, which cannot possibly exist, must be found by the two of us, who cannot possibly search for it.

When we visit the school, we are excited by the excellence of the teachers: we sit in on a science class taught by Mr. Neiderman, who is wonderfully energetic and smart. The students are studying the structure of the atom, jumping out of their seats with questions and answers. In a social studies class, a wonderful young teacher, Ms. Ajami, discusses the plague as a way to understand the breakdown of feudal society. We talk with the principal about the goals of the school and about safety, given the known drug problems in the neighborhood. We set up an interview for Zach. As we leave the building, we encounter some boys from another school that is housed within the same building. They are on the verge of a fight, and the situation seems very volatile. Normally, we would talk to the principal to clarify the relation between the two schools. But nothing is normal now, and we simply become afraid.

As David and I talk, I begin to understand how much he has identified with Zach as a child whose mother is sick. After all, a few years after David's mother died, David was having trouble in second grade. He claims that, when he called his teacher, Mrs. Cush, "Mrs. Pincushion," she told him never to speak again in class, so he stopped participating. I imagine the situation was more complicated than David remembers but, when Alex married Sophie, they moved David from a public school to the private school where Sophie was a teacher. David felt protected and loved in his new school. It's hard for David to realize that Zach is not as young or fragile as he was when his mother died; and I have not died yet. Zach is flourishing in the public school he attends now and is resistant to the idea of going to private school. David is struggling with his own vulnerability.

The week before my final chemo cycle we take our trip to Sag Harbor for two nights. On Friday evening we order pizza for the kids and David and I go down the road for a seafood dinner. I actually feel some excitement at the prospect of chemo ending; David and I talk as if we will have a future, planning Thanksgiving and Christmas. In the morning I wake early and walk into town to buy the newspaper, juice, coffee, and muffins. I like being up before David and doing something for him for a change. After eating breakfast, we find a rocky beach on which to walk and skip stones. As I watch David and the children playing with each other, healthy and lively, I feel sad and quickly become distraught. The scene tears me apart. David comes over to me and we walk. I cannot explain my upset but am concerned that it's another day on which I won't protect the kids from my fears.

While David and Molly go off to play, Zach sits near me on a big rock. He asks how I am feeling and wants to know some things about my childhood. The tenderness with which he attempts to make intimate conversation is touching, and I begin to feel better. Then Molly and I gather pebbles for her collection, filling up the car with our bounty. I laugh at how, like me, she is comforted by having as her own these concrete, beautiful objects.

When my study group meets in October, Laurie is still at Sloan-Kettering. We have given up the pretense of discussing cases or professional literature and are now functioning as a support group for those of us who have cancer. This time, the other members of the group encourage me to talk, and I become clear about the ways in which I am maintaining a distance from my family, for fear of feeling how deeply attached to them I am, lest I lose them. Each of us in this group has struggled with illness and death. How do we choose to stay alive, knowing there is death? We each have our ways of managing, but none of us really knows the answer. The best we can do is lend each other support.

To my last treatment I bring flowers and try to express my gratitude to Marta and Dr. Moore, but I feel too sick. Marta introduces me to another woman who is also finishing chemo today. She nearly quit in the middle but was persuaded to finish. She looks as if she's been through hell and feels even less relief than I that chemo will soon be ended—too exhausted to care, I'm sure. Even here, in public, she cannot hide her rage and bitterness; she's suffered too much.

Chapter eight

The Journey Back

It's been two and a half weeks since my last chemo, but I feel no better. I almost cancel today's date with a friend who has wanted to take me out for lunch. She's not always the most understanding person, but I decide to go anyway in an attempt to propel myself back into ordinary life.

We meet in SoHo in a small, quiet restaurant, and I immediately begin to talk about myself. I'm feeling very needy and a bit out of control of my feelings. My friend tells me about the old people she works with as a visiting nurse, and how much harder it must be to be sick if you are elderly, because then you really know that you are going to die. Doesn't she know that I also feel I'm dying? And I have young children. She rambles on, and I sense my rage building. I try to explain the sense of mortality I live with, but she tells me that I sound like her depressed mother. I'm stunned by her insensitivity and cut the lunch short to go home. I call Bonnie, who says many kind things to me: Of course I'm depressed; I have been through so much; it will take time to get back to normal. But I feel deeply disturbed all day: my lunch friend has confirmed what I'd begun to suspect—that the statute of limitations has run out for me. No more displays of distress allowed.

I have a terrible night. My dreams are filled with barely disguised replays of my lunch conversation. This is the part of cancer I loathe the most. I hate that I am so worn down that I can't even fake being good natured, that I am so demoralized that the slightest hurt reverberates for days. I have no sense of humor; nothing rolls off my back. I am no fun to be with. Others don't want to be with sick people, unless they are noble, long suffering, and silent about their illnesses.

I wonder why I am still so upset now that the chemo is over, why I am not getting on with life and the future. Perhaps the fact that this is my second cancer accounts for my anxiety. I could believe myself cured once, but twice? Perhaps it's that I believe it's only a matter of time before cancer reappears. Or perhaps everyone feels this way after such an ordeal, and cancer is simply not over when it's over.

I also realize that, although the diagnosis, the early decisions, and the treatments were horrendous, I was not as tired as I am now. My body has been cut up, poisoned, and parts killed off; my psyche has been assaulted. The difference between the beginning and the end of chemo is like that between a soldier going to war, brave and committed, and returning, beaten down by the horrors suffered.

It's October 25 and I have an appointment with Dr. Cody. While I wait, I get on the scale. It reads 138. I strain to understand what this means; the numbers do not register. I normally weigh 113 pounds. At first I can't seem to subtract the numbers; it's too upsetting. How could I, who am vigilant about my weight, have gained 25 pounds, as much I did with each pregnancy, without being aware of it? As I begin to absorb the reality of these numbers, I have to admit that I'm rounder at the middle and that my skirts have been too tight.

During my exam, I ask Dr. Cody if there is any problem in examining a breast after reduction. He doesn't generally recommend breast reduction, he replies, but he concurs with Dr. Moore's reasoning that a reduction affords a way to look at the tissue in the second breast. The procedure should not interfere with his examining that breast for lumps. Only after I leave do I realize my confusion. What did he mean when he said that he does not generally recommend breast reduction? Why did he send me to a plastic surgeon who acts as if breast reduction is almost a given? Then again, what plastic surgeon wouldn't recommend plastic surgery? I was not exactly thinking critically at the time of my decision.

Many people have reconstructive breast surgery, I know, but I increasingly wonder why. This decision has always seemed strange to me—having this foreign object, this balloon, inserted into my body so that I can pretend to have a breast. People report feeling better about themselves afterward, and I reasoned that I would feel more comfortable wearing a T-shirt or bathrobe in front of the kids. But I see now that I would have grown comfortable with my body even without reconstruction. Still, I've made my decision and I'll live with it. I try to console myself with the advantage of having the tissue in my second breast analyzed. At least this rationale is better than my wish to make my breasts match.

When David calls about coverage, the insurance company approves the implant surgery but not the reduction on the other breast. What does this mean? Are all women who decide on breast reduction, so commonly recommended by plastic surgeons, paying for it themselves? Is the insurance company confirming my own belief, that this surgery is unnecessary except for reasons of vanity? Then again, shouldn't one be entitled to a little vanity at this point? David nevertheless convinces the insurance company that the purpose of the breast reduction is simply to avoid a second mastectomy. Surprisingly, they accept this cost-cutting argument, and I am free to proceed with cutting up my other breast.

As I contemplate surgery, I reason that, if Dr. Breckman reduces my present breast to a size B and I then manage to lose twenty-five pounds, my size-B breast will shrink to a size A, and I will certainly not have a matching pair. David has no idea what I'm talking about, or, rather, he thinks I'm crazy and so makes no attempt to follow my reasoning. I try my logic on a few friends, who become extremely uncomfortable about the way that I am discussing the dissection of my breast. I finally speak to Laura, who listens carefully and says, "Of course, I see what you mean. You need to lose the weight before surgery if you can." I exercise, eat well, avoid fat and find that I lose fifteen pounds easily.

It's a crisp November morning and David, Zach, Molly, and I get dressed for the bar mitzvah of Jan's younger son, Jake. I love events that mark the next generation's maturation and call on them to present themselves as principled, thoughtful people. It's been a month since my final chemotherapy treatment, and I feel much healthier now, though any tiredness ushers in the familiar, sick, chemo feeling. I seem especially conscious of my breast this morning as I dress in a black suit that fits more snugly than it had. Zach wears a suit that I bought for him last week. At the time, I was proud of our purchase, but I see now that he looks as if he's wearing his father's suit. I wish he looked better so that I could feel that I had done better.

We arrive in Brooklyn early and find a diner to have breakfast together. Molly dances all the way because she's wearing a good dress. At the synagogue, we are greeted by Fred, who tells me how great my hair looks and then begins to backpedal when he realizes that it's a wig. I enjoy the service and note that the period of my breast cancer treatment has been bounded at each end by a bar mitzvah.

I watch Jan all day, knowing what this event means to her. It's been three years since her mastectomy and chemo. She has moved on to other concerns, though I know she does not take her presence here for granted. Her sisters have come, one whose husband recently died because of an undetected medical problem. Her father lost his wife a few months ago. Both he and Jan's sister are in new relationships. This family is a testament to survival. At the reception Zach works hard at looking relaxed, and Molly finds some girls with whom to giggle and dance. Jake has a great time with his many energetic thirteen-year-old friends.

I ask Jan to introduce me to her friend who has breast cancer and will begin chemotherapy with Dr. Moore next week. This is not the first time I'm drawn, in the midst of a party, to someone with whom I can discuss cancer. A strange impulse, I think. I once spent an hour at a family reunion discussing with my cousin's daughter her treatment for Hodgkin's disease. Jan's friend is a tall, attractive woman with thick, curly, blond hair; she tells me about her recent surgery and her difficulties in dealing with this cancer as a single woman.

I would like to help her, but she seems to have worked everything out already. She will begin chemotherapy while finishing her radiation treatments. She plans to work throughout and not be sick. I envy her confidence, recalling that, at her stage, I was much more pessimistic about my ability to cope. I try at least to offer her my now familiar advice about wigs, but she is not interested. She's already spoken to her hairdresser, who promises to make her a wig from her own hair if she saves it. Even in this respect, she seems more competent than I: if she must wear a wig, it will be of her own hair, not an artificial one like mine. I picture myself trying to collect the fallen strands of my hair from my pillow, the back of the couch, and the bathtub. Although the picture is ludicrous, her determination is admirable.

I am reminded of another woman whom I met in Dr. Moore's waiting room. She was so anxious about looking at wigs that I offered to accompany her. We went to Bits & Pieces, where she tried on a wig exactly like mine except in a darker color. She hated it. She said that she looked just like her mother, which was a bad thing, I gathered. She went on and on, describing why she could never wear it, while I sat there wearing a replica of the very wig upon which she was heaping her disgust. She left with fortified determination to keep her hair from falling out. I admire the refusal to accept this final humiliation. But I am hurt and angered by the indifference of these women to my feelings and by their presumption that, through an act of will, they can avoid what I couldn't.

I have been of no help to either woman, but I'm not sure why. At the time of my radiation treatments, Dr. Rosenthal asked me to visit a young woman who had been diagnosed with first-stage Hodgkin's disease. My visit seemed only to upset her; I represented her worst fear, and she didn't want to hear what she wasn't ready to face. Nor did Jan's friend want to hear a version of the experience that differed from the one she planned. And perhaps she was right in a way. She needed to preserve a sense of control and wait for her own experience to unfold; she could not worry about my feelings when she needed all her energy to survive.

Still, it's profoundly disappointing to have such difficulty in relating to other women who are being treated for breast cancer. I expected a closeness, at least a bond of fellow misery, but cancer does not guarantee a friendship any more than being a mother guarantees that one will get along with every woman at the playground. Perhaps the emotional devastation leaves one unable to take advantage of the chances for closeness. We are all too needy to attend to each other; it's a feat simply to keep ourselves going.

Each woman takes her pain in small doses, when she is ready. The doctors know this when they assure us that we'll be fine in surgery or on chemo. They let us discover what happens. And each person does react differently: one woman finds the idea of a wig intolerable but seems unworried about a recurrence; another thinks nothing of the wig but rails against the fatigue; still another accepts the nausea but hates the depression.

I go to see Dr. Breckman on November 16 for a pre-surgery visit. His nurse, the one who plays golf with him, is more authoritative than chatty this time. She examines me thoroughly, takes my pulse and my blood pressure, and listens to my lungs. She tells me how pleased I will be with the results of the surgery. I should not wear an underwire bra, exercise my arms, or lift anything for six weeks after the operation.

Dr. Breckman comes in. I've actually grown to like him. He's sorry that he could not do the surgery on the Wednesday before Thanksgiving, as I had requested, so that I would miss less work. The surgery now is scheduled for Wednesday, December 1. He looks briefly at my breasts, shows me where the incisions will be, and explains that he has devised a new way to cut so as to leave one less scar. I point out that the implant never expanded fully on the inside area of my breast. If he could move it in a bit, my breasts would be more symmetrical and I could have some cleavage. He'll try, but he thinks the radiation treatments have made the skin there less elastic. We also discuss my nipple. Because of the reduction, my nipple will no longer be in the center of my breast, so he would like to move it. This is too horrible to imagine. The notion of cutting off my nipple and sewing it back on somewhere else is grotesque, and to do so would be wrong, I think; agreeing to it seems like self-mutilation. But I can't leave it off center either, so I agree. I will probably lose sensation in that nipple, he tells me. Because sex is the farthest thing from my mind, I don't object. But there will be another loss to mourn.

Will the permanent implant be hard and appear stuck on my chest like the temporary one? I have chosen a size B implant, not a C, like my real breast size, because my frame is small and I am short waisted. Because the temporary implant feels big, I sense that a C would be too large. I don't need a giant breast sticking straight out. The nurse thinks that the implants have arrived, he says, but he'll call the hospital to double check. Dr. Breckman tells me that he was once in surgery when an implant broke and there was no extra on hand. He had to use a slightly different one, and the patient was so angry that she called every day for a year to scream at him. Now he orders two of everything. This story does not reassure me, nor does the fact that he's taken no measurements.

It is November 17 and I'm dressing to go out with David to a reception given for friends on the publication of their book. I realize that, despite months of looking in the mirror while I adjust my wig or put on make-up, I have not really looked at myself. I close the door of the bathroom off our bedroom, and I look hard at my reflection in the mirror. I see my mostly bald head, my many scars, and my breast in all its inflexible roundness. I look tired, old, mutilated. I try to absorb the reality of what my body is like now, and I feel, at this remove from treatment, not just the humiliation but some deep sadness about all that I have suffered. Yet I also feel that I can accept this body, even love this body that has been hurt so much, as I would love any wounded creature. And I know that when my hair grows back and I get stronger, I will give little thought to these battle scars.

Before we leave, my mother calls and talks about the weather, so I know something is wrong. Finally, she says, "Do you remember the mole on Chris's leg that she had biopsied last week?" I feel the bottom falling out of my world again. Of course I remember that mole, and I am flooded with all the fear I had glimpsed but not allowed myself to feel when Chris mentioned it. My mother tells me that it is a melanoma, a malignant skin cancer. The doctor will remove more tissue from the area surrounding the mole; he's optimistic that this measure will take care of it. She tries to reassure me, but I hear the worry in her voice. How much can she take?

The news stuns David, who keeps repeating that this is unbelievable, that Chris already has had too much to bear. The one person I know who had melanoma died very quickly. Chris herself is remarkably calm when I call her. There's no sense getting upset yet, she claims. She's already read extensively on the subject and knows that radiation and chemotherapy are possibilities, though maybe not for her because of her previous medical problems. We talk intimately, so similar in our problems yet so different in our ways of coping. I tend to home in on the worst possibilities and work them over and over in my mind. She, after an initial fit of rage, a few plates thrown against the wall, tries not to think about possible horrors to come. We are again having surgery the same week. When I had my mastectomy last April, she had a hernia operation. Jim jokes in the background about taking back the trophy from David for most long-suffering and heroic son-in-law.

On Friday, David and I are looking forward to a weekend alone, a gift from David's parents, who are eager to be with Zach and Molly. While David takes them to New Jersey, I keep the appointment that I scheduled with Dr. Moore. It becomes clear that I was mistaken about the need for this visit before the surgery, but I'm glad to see her anyway. I tell her about Chris. She assures me that my sister is likely to be fine, as is her sister who had a melanoma last year. We talk about our families, and I tell her that I'm the oldest of six and that I went to a Catholic girls' high school in Buffalo, to a Jesuit college, and then to graduate school at Harvard. She also is the oldest, and she grew up in New Jersey, where she attended a local Catholic high school, and then went to Smith. She was invited back to her high school a few years ago to give the commencement address in which she talked about the accomplishments of the other women in her class. She'll send me a copy. Of course this woman would not talk about her own accomplishments but would honor other women. She speaks with the utmost respect about women with breast cancer, who are able to manage the disease alongside the demands of jobs and families. I love the fact that she, whom I presumed to be an upper-class Protestant, turns out to be a Catholic-school graduate like me. I have finally found a woman with a background like mine who is a professional in New York. A role model. I guess it's never too late, and I chuckle when I think that she does look like my mother. As I prepare to leave, we return to business. She'll call the lab on the morning of my surgery to make sure that the tissue taken from my right breast is tested. She will see me again in three months.

I'm amused at the great pleasure I derive from this brief exchange. As a psychotherapist, I am careful about sharing personal information with my patients, so as to interfere as little as possible with the projections that they bring to their experience of me. But learning about Dr. Moore's life does not interfere with my projections. I cull from the information what I need to compose my particular picture of her. If reality contradicts that picture, I simply ignore it.

I meet David at the Paris Theatre to see *Remains of the Day*, having with me the tickets I bought before my appointment. The line extends down the block. David is near the end of it and worried that I will be late. I relate the details of my visit. He's clearly delighted that I'm in such a good mood.

We settle ourselves in front-row, balcony seats. Underneath my excitement about the weekend, I note a substratum of tiredness. When the movie begins, I become caught up by shots of the beautiful English countryside. Luckily for David, there's also a subplot about the Nazis. After the movie we walk over to a small French restaurant on West Sixty-eighth Street called La Boîte-en-Bois. We're seated at a tiny table, very close to other tables on each side. The room is overheated, and I feel claustrophobic. My rising desire to be home in bed collides with my wish to have a nice weekend with David. In other times, I would have loved the intimacy of this restaurant, but tonight I feel the room pressing in on me. I'm vaguely aware that I'm searching for someone to hate. We're headed for disaster, and David knows it. If I'm finding fault with everything around me, he's next.

This past week when I was trying to talk to David about some worry of mine, he told me that he was sorry but he couldn't handle hearing any more, that it took all his energy to maintain a semblance of normalcy for the kids. His exhaustion was written on his face and his depression in the way he carried himself. I vowed to pull myself together.

But I'm sitting here at dinner and failing already, unable to rise above my inner turmoil, hating myself for failing, yet convinced that it's David who views this as a failure. He's a character in my drama without having auditioned for the part. I want to scream at him, Why did you bring me here and why do you expect me to act normal? But I know that these are crazy thoughts, that this dinner plan was mine, as is the expectation that I act in a normal manner. Instead, I play out my inner battle: "I'm sorry I'm being so impossible. Maybe we should leave." "Fine," he replies. I say, "You want to leave because you're furious at me for being such a mess." And on it goes.

Finally, we order and I begin to calm down. I enjoy the salad of greens, goat cheese, and a garlic vinaigrette. We converse a bit, and then I lapse into my private world. I should not be here, I don't feel well. I'm not ready to resume life, and I am going to spoil the weekend. Later, I repeat the drama of indecision at home, wanting to have sex but needing to sleep. I dream about my sister and wake up realizing how worried I am about her. Living under a storm cloud, I can imagine only a downpour, never a clearing.

On Saturday we sleep late and David brings me coffee. Because the day is unplanned, we need to make decisions, but even the simplest choices overwhelm me. I don't know what I want or would enjoy. I know only that something's terribly wrong and I want to feel better. David is exasperated at my expectation that he will know what I need even though I don't. We finally decide to call our friends David and Zina, who drop everything to have breakfast with us.

They offer us the warmth and caring that neither of us can offer the other, and we begin to relax. The conversation turns to schools for our children, and we're relieved to be in something resembling our old, normal life.

David and I then go to lower Manhattan to do some Christmas shopping. I tire quickly and lapse again into indecision about what to do next. We settle on a movie in the afternoon. We choose *My Last Concubine;* a movie that makes *Remains of the Day* seem like a comedy, it is a horrifying story of sadism and betrayal in China under successive governments. Just what we need. We then grab a quick dinner before heading for Madison Square Garden to see the Knicks play.

The game is clearly a mistake for me. I've barely been out in the world, and I feel assaulted by the big crowd, the loud music and announcers, and the lights. Madison Square Garden has been David's haven, a place where he has been able to be distracted over the past few months, and I am here to spoil it. I sit moodily, knowing that David's exasperation with me is mounting. Why am I so enraged now, and why at him? Why was I better able to manage gruesome treatments and months of side effects? I am subjected to an endless stream of cascading, tumultuous feelings. I want to be close yet I push David away; I love him yet I attack him. I feel distraught beyond words, and it crosses my mind that I will make myself sick. Am I falling apart because the kids are away? Because of the cancer? Because my sister might die?

I take an Ativan and sleep the kind of sleep that comes from being totally spent. On Sunday David and I slog through my feelings of anger to find what's underneath it. I see now that I had so wanted to pull myself together, to ease his burden, that I had not admitted to myself how devastated I was by David's inability to listen to me, how abandoned I felt when he told me he'd reached his limit, how enraged and envious of his right to opt out of this misery. I realize that I've been trying to be finished with my pain prematurely, that I'm still terrified for Chris, outraged that the gods or fate or biology continue to visit their wrath on my family, nervous about my impending surgery. David assures me that he does not expect a transformation, that he knows it's not over yet. I let him hold me, finally, my lover and not my enemy. We pick Molly and Zach up early, knowing that it's time to end this weekend alone. I try to forgive myself for having ruined a good time. I'm beginning to realize that the end of chemo is not the end. It will take me a long time to heal, and I need to trust that eventually, in my own good time, I will return to normal.

We have a good drive to Buffalo for Thanksgiving. After six hours in the car, we stop at a motel and have dinner. Zach is in a particularly talkative mood. I ask him something about a girl whom I know he likes; he acts annoyed at my prying but relates the saga of his week. It seems that he had decided to ask Lisa to go out. All his friends urged him on, but he couldn't do it. He tells us how scared and nervous he felt and how determined he is to ask her out after vacation. We learn that "going out" has nothing to do with going anywhere but means being identified as a couple, what "going steady" used to mean.

I treasure this moment with him, so like our return from camp. He's a child who talks when he's on the road. He tells us that he really wanted to discuss this with us, but it felt too private. He also tells us about a girl at camp last summer who agreed to go out with him but, after thinking about it for a day, changed her mind. I silently thank him for supplying a missing piece of the puzzle of the past few months, of why he often seemed distracted and in his own world. It wasn't just my breast cancer; in addition to basketball, he had girls on his mind. Dr. Moore was right. "Your children will be fine."

The reunion with my parents is poignant yet familiar. They're clearly relieved to see me in person and looking fairly healthy. My mother comments favorably on my wig, but there's no discussion of breast cancer. We talk about the new babies and plans for the weekend. I think I now know why I was so anxious all week. I was worried that I couldn't keep myself together for my parents. I see that I don't need to act a part for them, and I can relax.

We spend Thanksgiving together at Chris's home. She and Jim have worked hard to make a beautiful meal on our behalf. My other three sisters and their families arrive, and we meet my two new nieces. It's a joy to see my sisters bask in their new motherhood. Zach and Molly are ebullient. They love coming to Buffalo where, they imagine, the entire family is always gathered together at a party, the cousins playing endlessly with each other. After dinner on Saturday we prepare to leave, all of us knowing that Chris and I each have surgery this week, mine simply for reconstruction, Chris's for the melanoma on her leg. All surgery is complicated for her; to prevent too much bleeding during surgery, she must stop taking her blood-thinning medications, but she then runs the risk of a blood clot. As I hug her, my eyes fill with tears, but she lets me know not to open the floodgates. We laugh to keep ourselves composed.

Ordinary Life

I expect no surprises with this operation, and I count on little interruption in my life. I will work Monday and Tuesday, then take off until the following Monday. I expect to recover as quickly as last time. Getting ready for the hospital now seems a routine. Jerry will take Zach and Molly to school. Adrienne will stay with them in the evening until David returns. I tie up the loose ends at work, and call a colleague to whom I need to make a referral. She herself turns out to have a precancerous condition in her breast and has been quietly living with the threat of cancer.

On Wednesday morning David and I take the usual taxi to the usual hospital for the usual admitting procedures. After I change and settle down in the waiting room, I get up at least six times to go to the bathroom. A distraught mother watches her baby being wheeled off to surgery. David and I acknowledge that things could certainly be worse than they are for us. Dr. Breckman stops by briefly and arranges to talk to David after the surgery. I feel as if I am merely the body.

When I'm called, David again accompanies me to the elevator, and I once again walk through the towering double doors on the surgical floor. But this time, instead of being taken to the operating table immediately, I'm ushered to another, smaller waiting room where a nurse checks some information with me. Two other women are brought in, one of them, tall, freckled, and very worried. I hear that she is going to have a lumpectomy and sense that she wants to keep to herself in order to marshall all her resources for surgery.

The other woman is in her fifties. She is scheduled for gynecological surgery but seems to have only a vague idea about what they will do to her. Because she's been in pain, she simply wants it over. Her insurance company won't pay for her to stay overnight, and she's worried that her daughter won't come on time to take her home. She talks mostly about her granddaughter. I'm grateful for her volubility and glad that I don't have to go home today, despite my aversion to hospitals.

The nurse takes me to the operating room, where I meet the other nurses, the anesthesiologist, and the interns. Dr. Breckman arrives, says hello, and spends some time talking to an intern about my situation—previously treated for Hodgkin's disease; stage-one breast cancer; left breast mastectomy; no lymph node involvement. He explains that he will remove the breast expander, insert the permanent implant, and reduce the right breast. They're learning the things about breast cancer that I've learned from books. I wonder if they have any idea of how little this information really teaches them about this disease. And I wonder if they want to know.

Dr. Breckman has me sit on the side of the table, measures my breasts quickly with a ruler, and asks how tall I am. It's a relief that he is seriously considering exactly where this "breast" should be placed. I am preoccupied with the thought that this group of male doctors will have me sit up during surgery to ensure that they get my breasts even. How else will they tell? There I will sit, a drugged forty-four-year-old woman, wearing a flimsy surgical hat over my sparse hair. Soon the anesthesiologist rescues me from my thoughts by inserting the IV into the vein in my arm.

回

This time the scene in the recovery room is a little more vivid. I'm in a bed at the end of a long room, and the woman next to me moans continuously. An attractive, middle-aged nurse pays considerable attention to me. I feel the same relentless, pounding pain as before, this time on both sides of my body; and I am again transferred to the cart for the trip to my room.

There are two beds in my room, and the other one is empty. David smiles as he tells me that, thanks to the efforts of Pam, my friend at Bellevue, I'm on the VIP list and therefore have this room to myself. He's managed to write an article on his computer while waiting for me to return. I sleep on and off. In what seems like a short time, David is ready to leave and I want to tug at him and beg him to stay, but I remember that he's been here all day; he should be with Molly and Zach.

The night is very bad, full of pain and drugs, vomiting and dry heaves. A night nurse attends to me carefully and encourages me on my first trip to the bathroom. She's a large, sturdy woman who lets me lean on her arm and rest when I become dizzy. She waits while I am in the bathroom. It's a pleasure to have good, solid nursing care, so different from my last experience here.

I feel horrible in the morning. I speak to David on the phone and tell him that I have not yet seen the doctors and I'm not even sure that I can make it home today. He responds that Jerry is planning to drive to the hospital with him so that he can stay in the car while David collects me. It's clear that I'm complicating David's plans and that he has no idea of how terrible I feel. I'm weaker than I was after my last surgery, and I have a throbbing headache and nausea. The thought of going outside terrifies me. David sounds concerned and tells me that he will come soon to be with me.

As I wait for the doctor, I am in a tug of war between my wish to go home and my fear that it might be dangerous to leave now. When Dr. Breckman visits, I can tell from his face that I look as terrible as I feel. He checks the wounds. I avoid looking at my body while he removes one drain. He does not oppose my desire to go home, probably recalling my aggressive campaign to be released quickly last time, but I can tell that he thinks I'm crazy. In a way I wish he would tell me to stay. But I'm not ready to stay either. He suggests that I see how I feel later and decide. "You mean I don't need to check out by eleven?" I ask. "No," he replies, and I assume this privilege comes with my new VIP status.

David arrives and tells me about the kids. Our moods do not match at all today, and I sense his disappointment in finding me such an emotional mess. He doesn't know what to say, so he reads the paper. I decide to see whether more sleep will help. I eat something at lunch and begin to feel a little better. I sleep again until two o'clock, when I feel well enough to go home. David helps me to the bathroom so that I can wash and brush my teeth. I snap at him, feeling that he's distracted and oblivious to my turmoil, frustrated that it's so hard for me to move about. He snaps back at me, letting me know that its unfair to blame him.

I realize that I should call Dr. Breckman about having the other drain removed before I leave, because I won't be seeing him for five days. His secretary relays the message, and soon a young, female plastic-surgery resident arrives from the operating room to remove the drain. She works carefully, explaining how the wound will heal and how I should wash until Dr. Breckman takes the bandages off. I feel old in the presence of this young female doctor. I wonder why she has chosen to specialize in plastic surgery and surmise that she wants a family and controllable working hours. I realize that I would never impute such benign motives to the choices that male doctors make.

I dress carefully, putting a loose hospital bra over the wide bandage wrapped around my upper torso. I have little relationship to these breasts right now and barely a thought about the purpose of this surgery. I'm still groggy from the anesthesia, and I want to get home.

When he's parked the car, Jerry comes upstairs to pick us up. I'm glad to see him. This is the kidney dialysis floor, he discovered, nicely appointed because it is well endowed. When Jerry comments on the traffic, David launches into a description of an altercation he witnessed this morning between two cab drivers and then goes on to describe the morning traffic. Doesn't he realize that I can't relate to anything in the world, that rush-hour tie-ups mean nothing to me? The nurse goes over some last-minute instructions; then Jerry wheels me downstairs and out the door.

On Monday, I manage to see all my patients, but I still feel as if I've been hit over the head with a baseball bat; either the anesthesia or the morphine must have caused me to have this endless headache. The old, sick, chemo feeling has returned, and I'm depressed by my failure to bounce back quickly. My friends gently point out that I had surgery just a few days ago; but I had expected this recovery to be less traumatic than the last, a kind of afterthought, certainly manageable after chemo, and, because it seemed more cosmetic than disease related, easy to recover from. Now I understand that I was minimizing the fact that the knife cuts just as deeply, whatever the purpose of the surgery, and it will take time to heal.

On Tuesday Dr. Breckman removes the bandages and checks the wound. He makes it clear that I could have removed them myself, and I tell him penitently that the intern told me to leave them on. Why do I accept blame when I have done nothing wrong? This is my first view of my breasts, the event I have dreaded all morning. Finally, I look at them, objectively, as if these breasts are not mine. All swollen and stitched, bruised, black and yellow. They're grotesque. I am shocked at the terrible beating they have taken, and I can't believe that Dr. Breckman is expressing his satisfaction at how good they look.

He tells me the pathology report confirmed what he had observed—that the tissue he removed was healthy: there was no sign of any cancer or precancerous condition in my right breast. As always, I cannot take in this good news. I leave his office and wait for a cab, my heart pounding. I'm still shocked about my breasts. The right breast has stitches across the incision under the breast and from that incision upward through the center to the nipple. The nipple is sewn on with black thread, and the prospect of its actually attaching to the breast seems remote. Without the bandages, my breasts feel unprotected. I want to cradle them. I feel overwhelmed by sadness about what has happened to me; and, although I know that I will make this adjustment eventually, right now I can only weep.

David is ecstatic about the latest biopsy results. I seem to care less about the healthy condition of the tissue than about how these breasts look. David listens to my description of my horrendous breasts and wants to see them. Ranting about how I can't stand to look, I refuse to show them to him. Finally, his coaxing makes me laugh. I calm down and gather my courage to lift my shirt. He tells me that my breasts look fine and that, when they've healed, they'll look great. He thinks Dr. Breckman has done a good job. I adore him for loving these swollen, stitched, artificial, reconstructed, and reduced breasts.

On the following Tuesday I return to Dr. Breckman's office to have the stitches removed. He has to dig them out, it seems. It takes a long time for him to finish, but the pain is negligible. He tells me that he is fighting with the lab to release a copy of the biopsy results. It seems that the nurse mislabeled my right-breast tissue, and the technicians at the lab were confused about which breast it came from. He pointed out that there's only one breast, asking, "So what's the problem?" The lab still would not release the written results to him. We schedule another appointment in ten days.

That evening I learn that my sister's surgeon believes he removed all the cancerous tissue from her leg and she needs no further treatment. Although I'm tremendously relieved for her, the news only briefly alters my mood, so engrossed am I in myself and so hard is it for me to trust any good news right now. I'm completely discouraged that, two weeks after my surgery, I still feel exhausted and weak. I keep missing my deadlines for finishing the ordeal of breast cancer. The first was October 15, the day of my last chemo. I was sick for two weeks after that, but I expected to feel better by November. When I missed that deadline, I set my sights on the weekend before Thanksgiving, the one I spent alone with David. That was a disaster. Now it's December and I have still not recovered. It's hard to accept that what's already been nine months of trauma has not come to a definitive end. And it seems a cruel joke to feel this bad when objectively the ordeal is over.

Because I feel so out of control, I seem particularly intent on keeping the apartment tidy. I react to the kids' messes as if they are catastrophes, when in fact I'm maintaining the apartment at such a level of neatness that it would be impossible for two children to dismantle it, even if they tried. The fact that Molly and Zach scamper away from me like mice from a cat informs me of my anger. What is my problem? I'm done with chemo; I'm not vomiting; I'm not even nauseated. This is no Greek tragedy or even an Italian opera; this is just a bad soap opera.

I'm even finding it hard to get out of bed and go to work, and I wonder how I ever worked through the six months of chemotherapy, with a full schedule of patients and a family. Perhaps I functioned in the way my mother did when one of us, as children, was injured and needed to be taken to the emergency room for stitches or x-rays. She remained calm and efficient but, when it was over, she collapsed in exhaustion, finally feeling the impact of what she had just handled. Now I am aware of the toll that this disease has taken on me and on David; he still is unable to absorb my complaints and worries. I feel abandoned by him and continue to be critical of everything he does. He reacts angrily and does not soften, nor do I. The children are mirror images of us. As we explode, they explode. It's as if we are all in a war that won't end. I'm filled with self-loathing because I know that I am at the center of this; if I would get my feelings under control, everyone would calm down. But I can't.

The books that I read talk about a let-down after chemotherapy. But who could have imagined that it could be this bad and last this long? It's not, as the books say, that without my treatments I no longer feel that I am doing something constructive about cancer. I feel let down because I cannot seem to return to my life. How am I supposed to go on living and believing there's a reason to do anything? Life seems too fragile. Why can't I have my old, unaware, daily life back?

It's December 17 and I am scheduled to see Dr. Breckman at two o'clock. I imagine what I might say to him. "I hate these breasts," or "You did a good job; I just didn't understand how disappointing a good job would be." My breasts have healed now and it's clear to me that they are not like new. The implant creates a breastlike mound that sticks straight out and looks very odd from the side. It certainly does not angle down gradually like a real breast. In addition, as the swelling diminishes, I am left with ripples on the inside of my breast that compose half of my cleavage. The other breast, where Dr. Breckman avoided one incision, is not round on the bottom but is a little flat. The nipple has healed nicely, although it has no sensation. The implanted breast seems bigger than my own breast. Although technically it is a B, in reality it is at least a C. What if I had chosen a C? Despite my discontent, I don't feel like complaining. It was naive of me to believe that the result would be better than this.

Dr. Breckman is not thrilled with the ripples either. This is the problem with saline implants, he says. He could inflate the implant more to fill out the ripples, but it would be harder to the touch. I say, "No, thanks." Harder would be like a rock, and I refuse to have any more surgery.

Now comes the explanation about the second nipple. Most women find that the implant feels like a real breast only if a nipple has been made. What he would like to do is to take a strip of flesh from my thigh or from my belly, where I already have a long scar. He would fashion it into a "nipple" and sew it on the implanted breast. He would then tattoo the nipple a color that would match my natural one. It would be a simple procedure, performed in the office. I tell him that I'll think about it and call him at a later time.

Will I call? I have my doubts. I vow not to be taken in again by the promise of a "real" breast. It will not be real. It will be a ripply, fake breast with a fake nipple, falsely colored. I need no additions to this grotesqueness. The implant fills my bra and that's great. I won't wear clothes that accentuate my nipple. David accepts this nippleless, fake breast. If he dies, I'll probably never be with a different man. If I am, I'm not going to pretend that this implant is a real breast. Do women who have breast enlargements for cosmetic reasons actually pretend that their breasts are real? Would a man not know?

After spending a lovely Christmas eve with our neighbors, we rise early to board a plane for California to visit our friends Gina and Fred and their children, who moved to a town near Berkeley from New York a year and half ago. We arrive late afternoon California time and rent a car to drive to their house. Hannah, who is Zach's age, greets Zach cautiously and Molly enthusiastically. Gabriel, born in Paraguay and adopted when he was an infant, has grown into a happy toddler. We feel cared for immediately by Gina and Fred and share a wonderful turkey dinner with them. They're delighted to see me in one piece. After dinner David and I talk with Gina and Fred while the children play in another room; they hear how frustrated and angry at each other we are. Although they knew that we were suffering, they had no sense of the degree to which we had unraveled. Now they see it. We sleep deeply and then spend a leisurely morning in the house. While Gina and Fred look after the children, David and I take a vigorous walk around a nearby reservoir and discover that we are already feeling better. We laugh and talk animatedly and are shocked to realize that we've not mentioned cancer all morning.

The first three days of our visit we refuse to be tourists, and we simply relax and recuperate in the house and its immediate surroundings. David and I are acting as if we've just been released from prison—marveling at the light filling the house, the leisure for reading the newspaper over coffee, the pleasure of entire days visiting with friends. Gina and Fred tease us about our state upon arrival; that first night they had gone to bed very worried about what a week with us would be like, so they are greatly relieved by our present good humor. The four children play together from morning to night. Gabriel is the mascot. Hannah and Zach act like cousins and ignore their prepubescent feelings. Molly works hard to negotiate her position, competing with Zach for Hannah's attention and with Zach and Hannah for the role of Gabe's babysitter. We eventually take the children to San Francisco, where we ride the trolleys, watch street theater, and eat crabs, and then to Monterey, where we visit the aquarium.

Gina and I buy dried and silk flowers for our home-decorating schemes. We find some sales advertised and shop for clothes, an activity that I have not engaged in for a year. Because we wear the same size, we try on each other's selections. It's good practice to be in the changing room with her. She sees me in my bra, and I realize that she's the first person aside from David and Chris to see any part of my breasts since surgery. It's fine. I know her enthusiasm about everything I try on is motivated by her wish to help me feel comfortable about my body.

She encourages me to forego wearing my wig in their home, given that my hair is beginning to grow. We make sure that Hannah is comfortable with my very short hair, and David joins Gina in her enthusiasm for my new hairstyle. Although I hate people fussing about my appearance, I now bask in the attention. I know that by his compliments David is telling me how much better I look with hair than without, but I pretend that he means I actually look good. David and Gina urge me to go out in public without my wig, showing me photos of chic models with very short hair as further inducement. I point out that these models are seventeen, not forty-four; nevertheless, their support gives me courage enough for a trip to the supermarket without my wig. No one faints. But then again no one knows me. By the end of the week I stop wearing it entirely. I go from trepidation to relief, and I begin to think that in ten days I may be ready to return to work without my wig.

Gina and Fred take care of our children so that David and I can have another chance at a weekend by ourselves, this time in San Francisco. We eat Mexican food, ride the ferry, and talk. We are overjoyed to find that it takes no effort to enjoy each other. When we return the kids visit their favorite store and stock up on magic tricks, which they delightedly perform for us each evening. We are astounded to feel so good and so rested and to have redis-covered our ability to enjoy each other as a family. There is no way to express our gratitude.

Back in New York with the rest of the week off, I am free to embark on a minor redecorating project of the room I use as my office. I need to change my life, so I will change this room. I become absorbed in thinking about colors, fab-ric, and furniture, and I'm amused that I, who have felt so out of control, can at least determine what happens to this room. I watch myself, amazed that I am enjoying my activ-ities yet fearful that my feeling of well being and good health might vanish at any moment. How could I feel so much better? After nine months with little pleasure, with only the relentless demands of cancer treatment, ten full days, away from New York and from cancer, seemed to restore me.

I notice, happily, my renewed interest in my surroundings. I am someone who generally pays attention to details—to what my home looks like, to what I wear. During my treatments I barely straightened up the apartment; I never bought flowers. It was the same with my appearance; I gave little thought to my clothes. When I had Hodgkin's disease, I wore the same jeans and T-shirts day after day. I even discovered, well into my radiation treatments, that my neck was dirty: ostensibly, I was trying not to wash off the magic marker lines that guided the radiotherapist, but I wonder if I was also avoiding any contact with the site of my original tumor. Like my weight gain, my dirty neck was a testament to my high level of distraction, my need to avoid acknowledging the damage that had been done to my body and the accompanying feelings of humiliation.

I begin to pay attention to my office again. I shop for a rug and finally choose a Turkish one of bright oranges and blues. I hang new white curtains on the windows and arrange the dried flowers that Gina mailed for me from California. I buy three inexpensive black frames and mats for some beautiful photographs that Dimitia gave me. I feel exhilarated that I have the energy to shop in New York. I love how bright and airy the room feels, and the symbolism of making my room come alive does not escape me.

Nor does the manic nature of my activity. In the six months after my treatment for Hodgkin's disease, I wrote my Ph.D. dissertation, worked as a teaching assistant for a course in English literature and as a resident student advisor in one of Harvard's undergraduate houses, and wrote endless letters of recommendation for students. I also applied to masters' programs in social work, finally able, with the knowledge of life's fragility, to make the career change I had long contemplated but always dismissed. No longer did I need to justify not using my Ph.D. or explain how I could possibly enroll in yet another degree program. I know that manic activity can often be an attempt to ward off depression, but what's wrong with that, I wonder. At least my psychological defenses are productive.

Eventually there are no more closets to clean, and our apartment, at least, takes on a semblance of normalcy. For a while I am carried along by the good experience of our vacation, but a different kind of depression soon overtakes me. I no longer feel terrified all the time or preoccupied with thoughts of death. Instead I feel numb, lonely, aimless, disconnected from my friends, not able to be interested in anything. My life is the same as before my cancer—work, family, friends—but it feels like only the trappings of a life, without substance or meaning. I would have expected this depression to be less disturbing—ennui rather than terror—but it's not. It reminds me of the depression of my early twenties—so pervasive, without apparent cause, impossible to penetrate. I have often wondered if something in my life might trigger the return of those feelings. Now something has, and I feel only slightly better equipped than I was then to move out of this depression and to believe it will end.

Sometimes I am able to see that, although these feelings of depression seem to hit me from out of nowhere, they are generally triggered by a dream, a memory, something to do with cancer. Now I recall that last night I learned that the lesions in Estelle's brain are very large; they have affected her sight and hearing and have caused some paralysis and considerable brain damage. Arlene, her partner, struggles to admit that there is nothing more that can be done, that it's time to say goodbye. She sits for hours beside Estelle who cannot communicate with her in any way. I tell Arlene what Estelle told me two months ago— that she was so grateful to Arlene for all she was doing and wished she could find a way to thank her. Arlene wants to hear this over and over again, to hold on to any connection with Estelle.

I still do not visit Estelle. I feel like a coward, but my own equilibrium seems too precarious. I plan, with all the eagerness of one in need of a rationalization, to pay tribute to Estelle by my friendship with Arlene. If a conversation keeps me in turmoil all night, what would a visit to my dying friend do?

Often, though, I cannot connect my depression to any particular source. While doing errands or making dinner I may be overcome by a feeling of unbearable sadness. At night, I sometimes awaken to find that I'm gripped by the fear I battled during those nights of treatment. At other times the unrelenting sobs return for no apparent reason.

To my patients I look as if I am done with breast cancer. I've progressed from my wig to my own, very short hair. Some of them think that I look like a boy, others that I look beautiful; still others are too shocked to acknowledge this most recent, drastic change in my appearance. Most of them were glad that I took a vacation and saw it as a sign of closure on my breast cancer. We revisit their earlier experience of my cancer—their shock at my diagnosis, their fears, their anger. Some tell me that it remained hard to be a patient when what they really wanted was to take care of me, move into my home and cook, watch my kids. Many still struggle with how marginal they felt. Others appreciate my openness and marvel that we managed therapy pretty much as usual.

There were those who were ready to leave therapy but stayed on, thinking that their presence might magically guarantee my survival. Now we prepare for their departure. Some are angry that I didn't take time off to take care of myself, others that their therapy was so seriously interrupted by my cancer; they think I should have kept it to myself. This is hard to hear. I talk with a few patients about how distant they seemed in their reactions, as if they were unaffected by my illness, and we uncover the fears they could not then approach. My illness has become a touchstone for us, a shared experience that deepened our understanding of how these patients live, some more fearfully than they had realized, some more lovingly.

Feeling so tired and vulnerable myself, I find it hard not to take personally what my patients say. Some of them think I was incredibly strong during my treatment whereas others considered my illness a sign of my frailty and consequent inability to handle them. It's hard for me to avoid feeling grandiose about my heroism or ashamed of my fragility and to listen to what they are telling me about themselves.

I expend my energy on work, and when I'm done I'm hit by depression again. My friends are available to me, but when I feel most distraught I do not call them. Instead, I imagine I have been abandoned by them. The phone rings less often now that I have finished chemo, and I assume people are happy to be free of worry about me. Of course, I am the one who is out of contact; I am merely acting out what I feel inside—cut off, desolate, and alone with my experience.

I have been hesitant to set my hectic life in motion, to plan lunches with friends, to jog in the park, to attend professional meetings, to pick Molly up as often as I had in the past. I have an idea that I should reorganize my priorities—decide whether I want to work so hard, to find more time to write and to listen to music, to develop a more meditative stance, to give up my neuroses. Having railed against the notion that cancer is transformative, I am searching for a way to transform myself. Finally I realize that preserving time alone may not be the answer, and I begin phoning. I reach answering machines but no friends. Eventually people call back and I begin to set up dates for lunch and walks in the park, amused at the idea that in a few weeks I will be complaining that I'm too busy.

Chapter ten

Anniversary

Throughout January, I continue to fluctuate between normal life and desolation. Or perhaps, more accurately, I come to see that normal life holds happy days filled with family, work, and friends interspersed with days when I feel desolate and completely fearful of illness and death.

Pam has planned a party for me, inviting our old friends, the group from the picnic. Some are coming from as far away as Washington, and I am deeply moved. As I dress, I try to view myself as looking fashionable rather than looking like a cancer survivor. But with my breasts different and my hair so short, all my clothes look too big. I select some silk pants and a black velvet top. We meet at Pam's and my friends seem genuinely enthusiastic about my healthy appearance and they like my hair. Although it's strange to be celebrated for surviving, I do consider it an achievement. And, though I sometimes feel uncomfortable at parties, I eagerly let myself be embraced by the enthusiastic warmth of my friends.

Pam serves elegant appetizers and champagne. David makes a short toast to me, and I am moved not so much by his words as by his apparent joy at my recovery. At one point I catch David and Jerry looking at me and obviously commenting on me to each other. I know they are saying "Doesn't she look great?" and we exchange a laugh across the room. I know that they really mean, Thank God she's back. Thank God she is her old self. Thank God she is still with us and can enjoy life. Thank God for them, I think.

Molly is at home today, and we talk about when I was sick. Although she seems fine, at least on the surface, I've noticed that separations are more difficult for her now; she holds on to me a little longer before going to school, and she prefers sleepovers at our house. I ask what she remembers about cancer. She recalls the day I came home from my first hospital stay—how left out she felt when everyone was visiting and bringing me presents, how she cried and got angry at me, and how I then cried and snapped at her. Our recollections of that day are remarkably similar. She, however, recalls only the trauma and not the reconciliation.

She cries now as she tells me this, and I hold her and tell her how glad I was that she let me know how angry she felt because then I could fix things. I remind her that we spent more time together after that episode, that she brought me juice and climbed into bed with me to read her book.

Why am I surprised by her crying in my arms now? Did I really believe my illness did not touch her deeply? She tells me that sometimes at recess she would feel alone and think about me. And, "When you went to the hospital, Lucky wasn't enough; Lucky was just a stuffed animal and wasn't alive and I missed you." She relates losing her tooth in school and feeling excited about showing it to me at the bus stop, then remembering that Zach, not I, would meet her bus and walk her home.

And she tells me more—that she liked Daddy picking her up at the Y, but she sometimes felt envious of Rebecca, whose mother came for her. She tells me that it was hard to stay with other people as much as she did because things were different in other families. I let myself feel what it must have been like for her to have me so inaccessible, so absent from those places in her life where, I like to think, I had normally been so dependable. How bittersweet it is to know how much she needs and loves me. What if I have to leave her? What if I die?

One evening in February I talk to David about my discouragement at still feeling so depressed. I've been avoiding him in the past few weeks, trying to act as if I'm fine; so I'm surprised that we have a good talk. I tell him how hard yet unsuccessfully I am trying to fight my way out of depression. I wonder whether to join a cancer support group, call a therapist, talk to friends more often, or just wait this time out. David asks if I've thought about writing, and I'm surprisingly intrigued by the idea, though I had previously rejected it. Perhaps I have the energy now; perhaps I am reminded of how writing in my journal helped me through my very introspective adolescence; perhaps I'm moved by his thought that it might someday be valuable for me to have a record of this experience, even valuable for our children. Certainly I am encouraged by his healthy belief that it's worth a try.

My only hesitation is that I won't find a voice for my experience, a way to describe what often seems beyond words. I sit down a few hours later and begin, planning to ignore the search for a voice and simply to describe the events of my breast cancer as I remember them. In the next few days I produce a pile of written pages and find that I am not depressed. It's as if the writing relieves me of the burden of my feelings. Whenever I have a free moment, I write, and I find that, by remembering, organizing, and describing my experience, I am prevented from following every worry that comes my way. The writing is like a magnet that draws together all the stray parts of myself. That I feel creative in describing such a horrendous experience amuses me, and I am struck by the passion with which I approach the telling of my story. It feels as though I am writing to save my life.

Throughout March I continue to feel healthy and surprisingly free of my old demons. I work, exercise, and plan birthday parties for Zach and Molly, as well as a large party for David to which Harry and Laurie come, now that Laurie has completed her bone marrow transplant. She looks frail, having lost considerable weight; her short hair becomes her. She is beautifully dressed and as warm and generous as ever. Laurie and Harry stay late—each talkative, bright, and funny, remarkable in their ability to enjoy themselves and other people despite their ever present fear that Laurie's cancer will recur. Those of us who have been through this with Laurie know that this time together with her is the real cause for celebration.

Lately, Laurie and I have talked on the phone a lot, particularly about Laurie's sessions with her psychotherapy patients after a six-month absence. Laurie's task seems monumental. She is still healing from her very aggressive chemotherapy and surgeries. Her patients are reacting strongly to her radically changed appearance, but not always voicing their anger about her illness and their fears about her future health. Laurie is determined to help them say what they feel, which means hearing from them her own worst fears—that her cancer will recur and she will die.

As the first anniversary of my diagnosis approaches, I begin to feel shaky again. Although Dr. Cody told me to expect this reaction, I am not prepared for the intensity of my anxiety. Two news articles in the *New York Times* add to my worry. The first describes how a Canadian researcher falsified data on patients who were included in a major study comparing outcomes of lumpectomies and radiation with those of mastectomies. The experts quoted in the article too quickly offer reassurance that the results—that lumpectomies with radiation and mastectomies are equally effective—would be the same without these data. How can anyone be so cavalier about research that affects so many lives? But my outrage is somewhat muted by the knowledge that I have had a mastectomy; had I had a lumpectomy instead, I would now worry that the surgery had not been extensive enough. By creating the illusion that I am safe, I separate myself from women in potential danger— that is, from those who chose to have lumpectomies.

I cannot separate myself as easily from the article on tamoxifen, a medication that blocks the production of estrogen and seems to prevent the growth of estrogen-fed tumors like mine. Tamoxifen has been shown to improve survival by about 10 percent in postmenopausal women whose tumors are estrogen receptive. Although the drug's short-term side effects are minimal, its long-term effects are not yet known. The *Times* reports that recent research indicates a slightly higher than normal incidence of a particularly insidious form of uterine cancer among women who have taken tamoxifen. Some women have died, though only a very small percentage. Predictably, it takes time to calm myself after reading this article and to accept that I am simply playing the odds.

Because it is not yet clear that I am postmenopausal, Dr. Moore has suggested that we delay our discussion about tamoxifen until the fall. I'm relieved by the postponement of another decision and glad for some time to think. I hate the idea of more medication. Tamoxifen, which comes in pill form to be taken twice a day, may, like the drugs that I have taken, make me jumpy, nauseated, tired, and give me mouth sores. And it may increase the chance of uterine cancer.

Tamoxifen does seem to help prevent osteoporosis and heart disease, in addition to providing protection against breast cancer tumor growth. A friend who has been taking it for ten years says that it also prevents dry skin but may usher in hot flashes and weight gain. I could deal with hot flashes, but weight gain is a different matter. We're talking about a pill that I might take forever. Weight gain forever. I'd rather take my chances on breast cancer than be fat. I'm joking, of course, or am I? It's one thing to lose my hair and be nauseated temporarily, but to lose control of my weight forever? I talk to women on tamoxifen, none of whom have ballooned out of control. So we'll see in the fall. I wonder about myself; I must be feeling better if I am worrying more about my weight than about the possibility of uterine cancer. It's wonderful to be so distanced from my fears of a recurrence.

My pain this week is primarily due to my inability to feel. Numbness must be my version of holding my breath when faced with medical tests such as my mammogram next week. I recall a dream that I had when pregnant with Zach and waiting for the results of my amniocentesis. In the dream my body was encased in plaster and I could neither move nor feel. On Sunday I learn that Estelle has died and that the funeral will be on Tuesday. Although I cry a little, I still feel numb. I look forward to the funeral because I want to experience strong emotions again, to cry and mourn this friend who became sick after I did.

On Monday I see a new client who wants to discuss some difficulties she is having with her ten-year-old daughter. Only toward the end of the session does she tell me that she had a lumpectomy for breast cancer ten years ago, a recurrence in the other breast five years ago, and now a recurrence in her lungs. She will be informed of the treatment plan on Wednesday. I conduct the session professionally and only later, when talking to a colleague, do I realize that this is not a good situation for me or my client.

Yes, I can understand her. But how can I listen to an account of my worst nightmare week after week? How can I contain my own panic as I hear how this disease will not leave her? And how will I hear about her relationship with her daughter without thinking about Molly and me? This woman deserves to see a therapist who can keep straight whose experience is being discussed. Right now I am so separated from my feelings that I think I could actually handle the situation, but the tension in my body tells me that it would be at too great a cost. I will make a referral to another therapist.

I dream that night that Molly has a brain tumor. Last week I dreamt that Zach had cancer of the sweat glands. I follow my associations: cancer—glands—Hodgkin's disease—nodes—night sweats—sweat—adolescence—Zach. It seems that any mention of cancer, as in the session with the woman who has breast cancer, sends me into the land of worry.

It's Thursday, March 24, and the day of my first post breast cancer mammogram. I'm terrified and ask David to come along. Will the technician call me in again for more x-rays to get a clearer picture? I try to remember that my recent breast exam with Dr. Cody indicated no problem, that the tissue from my second breast was clear. But the ghost of Dr. Klauber rises again. There may still be cancer in the other tissue. Will this mammogram show something? Will I need to see Dr. Cody, have a biopsy, wait, go crazy again?

I fill out insurance and medical-history forms. This time I check "yes" next to each question—biopsy, mastectomy, scars. The form has a diagram of two breasts on which I must draw the lines of my scars. I keep repeating to David that I am terrified. The technician calls me, and I tell her that I've just finished chemo for breast cancer and am frightened that the mammogram will show something. I've gotten better at dragging out of medical workers the information or reassurance that I need. She is kind and makes the procedure as easy as possible. I only have one breast to x-ray, so the discomfort is limited. She squeezes my breast hard between the plates and tells me to take a deep breath while she goes behind the shield to push the button. Finished.

She tells me what a good job my surgeon has done on my breasts. She has seen some bad jobs. I'm amused that my breasts, strange as I find them, are a good job. I wonder what a bad job looks like. She tells me that I need to wait a few minutes while the doctor looks at the slides. I feel so anxious waiting that I resume my old frozen posture, as if bracing for disaster. I think about telling the technician that, if they find anything, she should inform David, not me—that I will lose my mind, tear up the room, tear out my hair. I begin to recite prayers—myself as a ten-year-old Catholic girl trying to ward off all bad things. I say the Our Father but realize that I prefer to speak to a woman and switch to the Hail Mary. Maybe someone in heaven can negotiate a change in fate. Maybe saying ten Hail Marys, or fifty, will at least take my mind off other things.

The technician comes out. Everything is fine. When I tell David, his body visibly relaxes. As I look at him, I see how worried he has been and I wish with all my heart that our life would return to normal. After I deal with the bill, we walk up Park Avenue, feeling ecstatic about this early spring day, this spring without breast cancer. The tension has left David's face, and I feel so relieved. David waxes philosophical, as he has since his own good medical check-up yesterday. "Life is like Russian roulette," he says. "You go through these check-ups over and over in your life, and most of the time everything is fine, but sooner or later it's not and you die." David's doctor told him that he sees many older women who had mastectomies twenty years ago. Now they're worried about their hearts. Maybe I will get to worry about my heart.

We walk across Central Park at Sixty-fifth Street, passing the playground where we often took Zach as a little boy. We are amazed that the slide is so small, not high and steep as we viewed it then through his eyes. We talk about taking the kids to Shakespeare in the Park in the summer. There will always be scares and doctors' visits. But there may also be life. As we walk up Central Park West and past the Dakota, we recall walks here together twenty years ago when David first introduced me to Manhattan. He entertained me with anecdotes about the history of New York, as he does today. We are back in our ordinary life.

A friend asks me to speak with her colleague who has just been diagnosed with breast cancer. One of her nodes was positive and her chemo will include Cytoxan, Adriamycin, and 5FU. I call to offer my support. I warm to her as soon as I hear her talk. She's Puerto Rican, forty-one years old, talkative, and honest.

She describes every traumatic step from finding the lump in her breast to having a mammogram, a biopsy, and a lumpectomy. She has what she calls "spells," crying, ranting, and raving spells, episodes with which I can certainly identify. Her story is poignant. As a teenager she was told by two doctors that she had fibroid tumors that precluded her having children. She spent twenty years having sex compulsively, trying to prove the diagnosis false, and married a terrible man because he already had a daughter and wouldn't mind if she failed to conceive. She went to psychotherapy for years in an attempt to accept not being able to have the child she wanted even more than a husband. A month before her cancer diagnosis, a gynecologist informed her that fibroids do not necessarily mean that one cannot have a child; there are things that can be done. In that single visit, the central problem on which she had structured her life was removed. Then her oncologist told her that chemotherapy would probably cause her to enter menopause. Even more than breast cancer, even more than chemotherapy, she resists and rails against a medically induced menopause that will probably end her hope for a child.

I really like this woman. My conversation with her is constantly interrupted by other calls and by people entering and leaving her house. I think she will be fine, perhaps because she is coping in the way that I coped and I am now fine. In her description of her experience I recognize my own—that she can't believe this is happening to her, that she wants out, that she hardly recognizes herself in her rage and frustration, that she feels she's driving everyone near her crazy. She tells me that, on the day she woke from her surgery, she read the article in the *Times* describing the flawed data in the Canadian study, and she began screaming for the doctors to take her back to the operating room immediately, that she wanted a mastectomy, to be rid of her breast, to take no chances.

The wife of a custodian in our building has a third-stage breast cancer—a large tumor and a number of positive lymph nodes. She is thirty-five and the mother of four children. Her husband is gentle and loving and keeps trying to cheer her up. Her boss will not guarantee her a job when she finishes treatment. He never even asks about her. She is in that dark, despairing place—feeling so incredibly sick that nothing else seems to matter. Her ranting is muted; she's angry but not sure that she's entitled to express it. Her doctor tells her that she can't possibly be that nauseated. She cannot imagine how she will arrange for her children's care and commute to the radiation treatments that she is soon to begin. She must take two buses from her home in the Bronx to a more remote part of the borough, and she must do it alone because her husband and relatives are working. I cannot penetrate her despair at all.

I speak to a friend's cousin who found a large lump in her breast and whose lymph nodes tested positive for cancer. She is preparing to fly to Seattle for a bone marrow transplant and is arranging for her sister and a friend to be with her. She expresses only optimistic feelings about her situation. She is determined to survive. Although her approach is certainly different from mine, I am now able to respect her determination. I do not require that she be like me.

I no longer feel so distant from other women with breast cancer, preoccupied by their better or worse prognoses or their different ways of coping. I am hungry for, rather than fearful of, their stories. I hear the commonality of our experience—the initial shock, the terrible decisions that have to be made, the emotional and physical pain. When I talk to these women, I know from the sound of their voices that they are alone in that other world where I have been. I know how faint my voice must sound to them.

If they could hear me, I would tell them what people told me: that I've returned to my life, that I think of breast cancer only once in a while and with less terror. I would tell them that I don't cry anymore, that I feel comfortable with my body and satisfied with the implant. My real breast is no longer flat on the bottom, nor is it disheartening to look in the mirror. I'm glad that I declined a second mastectomy. I now see my doctors as people, not as the receptacles of all my projected needs and fears. I go to my check-ups with less trepidation, and I even express my personality there, something I rarely did during my cancer.

I no longer feel depressed or expect that depression is lurking around the corner. The longer I feel healthy and life goes on, the more I relax. David is very busy lecturing, writing, teaching. I'm interested in work again, and I pick up the kids, shop, cook, and entertain friends. Zach attends public school and is extremely happy there; he does his homework with genuine enthusiasm and a newfound independence. Molly sleeps at her friends' houses and seems more relaxed. We are no longer an angry family.

David and I enjoy our time together again. We do the things we love—take long walks, browse in bookstores, just talk. We enjoy sex more than ever. We are thankful that our marriage survived my cancer, though mindful of the battering it has taken, and hopeful that we will have more years together.

I have not truly faced the prospect of my own death, though I have tried. I have faced many little deaths—the loss of my breast, of my fertility, of my innocence. I have felt dead to much of myself—to my feelings, to my family and friends, to the joy I normally feel in life. Now I am surprised at how alive I feel again. I have made no big changes in my life. At some point I simply decided to resume my life as it had been before my diagnosis. I glory now in ordinary life and the feeling of health. I expect that soon my appreciation will diminish and I will complain more. Then I will really be back to normal.

Last week as I walked the kids home from the school bus, Molly whispered in my deaf ear. I reminded her that I couldn't hear and said, "Isn't it funny that bad things always seem to happen to me on my left side." And I listed them. That evening I heard Zach say to his friend, "Everything happens to my mother on her left side. When she got Hodgkin's disease, the lump was on the left side of her neck. When she lost her hearing, it was in her left ear. Last year she had breast cancer on the left side. Now her left knee hurts."

I loved the confidence with which he stated these facts that explain nothing. His description of the location of my bodily injuries seemed to give him a sense that he understood what had happened to me. By describing my cancer in terms that limited and contained it, he could feel that he had a hold on the capricious disease that had threatened his mother's life.

Molly also remembers the comment. I am lying with her on her bed after reading to her and she asks me to tell her the story of my left side. At first I am baffled, and she says, "You know, how everything happens to you on your left side." "Oh yes," I say, "I lost the hearing in my left ear. I had breast cancer in my left breast. My left knee hurts." She adds, giggling, "And you're losing the hair on the left side of your head." I reply, "But, Molly, I'm not losing my hair anymore. Now it's growing in." Then she asks, "Is it over, Mom?" I ask, "Is what over, honey?" "Breast cancer," she replies. "Yes, Molly," I answer, "breast cancer is over."

Afterword

This is not the story I would have chosen to tell. Had my cancer led to my death, this is not the memorial I would have preferred to leave behind, nor is the morose, self-centered woman I describe the mother I would want my children to remember. In short, this is a difficult story to own.

Certainly, I set out to write the truth about my cancer while I was still in its grip. I was passionate in my resistance to telling the story that other people seemed to want to hear—of lessons learned, of cancer as a transformative experience. But having told my story, I now find myself startled by its fierceness, its raw and unrelenting character. I almost wish, when I read it over, that it left me with more of a feeling of transformation. There are other stories about breast cancer that would be easier to live with. Why, I wonder, couldn't I have written one of those? It's not my anger that I mind. I'm proud of my anger, at least when it's clean and direct, a response to injustice. But it's difficult to accept how mean spirited and lost I felt when I spoke from inside my illness.

Why am I surprised to find this angry Kathy Conway emerging from these pages when I know that I was angry during my cancer? Perhaps the experience of writing felt so good that I expected those good feelings to be reflected in the story. When I wrote, I felt creative, alive, still thinking, and productive—not deadened by the cancer or the chemicals. Somehow, writing transported me from that place of misery back to the ordinary world where I felt more like "myself." But the writing that transformed the experience of cancer for me did not result in a book about a transformed person.

Sometimes I would like to tell the reader that the person in this book is not really me. I'd like to go back and add those times when I was funny, when I was loving to my husband and children and understanding to my friends. Such moments rarely made a mark on my experience of cancer, just as the generosity of friends and loving times with my family seemed to have so little effect on my essential misery. Those "good" aspects of myself or my relationships seemed to carry no weight. I had become the misery I felt.

This is not my first attempt at an afterword. I wrote another in which I assumed the role of an anthropologist back from the field, reflecting on the behavior of people I'd studied, people dealing with illness in sometimes strange but ultimately well-intentioned ways. I spoke then in another voice in order to leave behind a different version of myself: wiser, more magnanimous, more self-possessed. I was trying, in a way, to take it all back, to undo the fact that this book describes me as I actually felt and acted then.

When I began to write, I felt some urgency because I knew that once I was outside the experience I would forget what the illness and desolation really felt like—as I had after Hodgkin's disease. I recognized that the better I felt, the more I might talk as if breast cancer had been manageable; I might even begin to believe it.

I doubt that I could write this book today. I no longer feel as raw as I did then. I see now that, in my own way, I was like those women who appear in public without a wig or a prosthesis and say, "Look at me. I have no breast. I have no hair. You must see what breast cancer is." I was showing that breast cancer is also this. feeling so horrendous and beaten up that you can neither fight nor demand that the world pay attention; you can only get through it, barely and ignobly.

For me, hearing the diagnosis of cancer meant entering a closed circle inside of which I was separated from my ordinary life, my ordinary self, from the very people I loved. Inside that circle I felt like a creature from a different species or, more accurately, one of the possessed characters in *Invasion of the Body Snatchers*. I looked the same, at least for a time, but my spirit had been taken away.

In my body, I had mindless, ruthless cells threatening to multiply ceaselessly and kill me. Even the chemicals intended to destroy them wreaked havoc. The most primitive emotions—terror, repulsion, blind hatred, and despair—seemed to overpower all positive or benign feelings. Only my anger at the threat to my life survived, and I held onto it for dear life.

Once I was inside that circle, my perspective changed: nothing seemed to matter much, except being sick. Activities that I had enjoyed disappeared from my life or lost their meaning. Friends who were generous (if sometimes insensitive) seemed only hurtful. The world outside felt unfamiliar and threatening in its normalcy; ordinary life like some idyllic state filled with innocent, fortunate people who did not have cancer.

I would have given anything to gain some distance from my cancer. But how could I, given that the cancer existed inside of me? My friends could. They could visit me, think of me, and then go about their business. They could still feel that they had control; that by eating carrots, avoiding stress, exercising, or meditating they could ward off cancer. I couldn't. The cancer was already in me. I was the threat, the one from whom they had to keep their distance.

People suggested at the time that I imagine myself somewhere else, at a beautiful place such as the beach, feeling healthy and calm; or in the future when cancer would be gone. But I couldn't. I knew that I was in my doctor's office receiving chemotherapy. I knew I was nauseated. My imagination couldn't perform such tricks, couldn't overcome what I was feeling in my body or even conjure up a time when the circle would reopen. I simply couldn't conceive of a time without illness. It seemed presumptuous to think that I would ever be cured and have a future of good health to look forward to. Why should I be one of the fortunate ones?

I did have a healthy year after my chemo ended, when life again felt normal, my days free of the misery of illness, though never completely free of the threat of cancer. With some distance, I began to view my breast cancer less as a departure from my life than as a part of it. In December 1994, when the enlarged node removed from my clavicle was shown to contain some scattered lymphoma cells, I once again faced an array of diagnostic tests—a bone marrow biopsy, blood tests, CAT scans—in a search for the disease elsewhere in my body. For a while I struggled against despair, but my new coping mechanisms soon collapsed, and the angry person of this book reappeared. To my horror I found that, even if ordinary life no longer existed without cancer, cancer still didn't include ordinary life. With cancer, life once again lost its complexity.

My doctors discovered no further evidence of disease and so decided to hold off on chemo and monitor me closely. This was an aggressive lymphoma; were the cancer still present, I would probably have developed symptoms within months after the diagnosis. Chemotherapy is effective in treating this type of lymphoma and my doctors believed that, if more cancer were found, the delay would not compromise the treatment's effectiveness. So far, no further cancer has been found.

Back in ordinary life again, I find that I view the experience of breast cancer differently, depending on where I am located in relation to it; and I understand that the emotional tasks that I face are different, depending on where I stand. When I wrote this book, cancer had taken over my life and I needed to tell the story of my ordeal. By the time I composed the ending, my view had begun to change: yes, breast cancer was miserable, but after the treatment I was returning to normal life. At that point I needed to bring the experience to an end, to end the book. Like my statement to Molly that cancer was over, completing my story was a way of willing the end, of drawing a line in the sand and saying, No more. This is the end of this experience with cancer. Of course, I knew that there can be no closure on this disease, but I needed to get on with life, as did my family.

During my illness I searched for narratives that would structure my experience and offer me a vision of the future in which breast cancer would end. I wanted to believe what my doctor said, that this was an acute episode, as was my Hodgkin's disease. I studied my diagnosis and statistical survival rates to find material with which to compose a story that had a future in which I would be healthy; and I tried to imagine the end of chemotherapy—I'll feel better in four days, in a week, when chemo ends, at Thanksgiving. None of this worked very well; I could believe in the end only when I felt healthy again.

When I am threatened once more by the possibility of having cancer, the experience looks as unmanageable and terrifying as ever. After my lymphoma diagnosis, I found this book and the portrait of the person I might again become unbearable. I could no longer see that cancer and its treatment could be a discrete episode in my life, only that it was a black hole into which I desperately feared being sucked, with no promise of escape.

At this remove from my illness, reassured by nineteen months of healthy life since the lymphoma diagnosis, I find that I can accept the story I have written—even my angry, whiney, critical self—because now I am the reader and she is the protagonist, the other, a character in the book. Although I can see her with all her faults, I do not completely identify her as me. I can even be compassionate and think that, of course, I was enraged, miserable, and self-centered; any behavior is understandable under those circumstances. Now I have the distance that so eluded me when I was sick.

This more benevolent attitude derives from the fact that back in ordinary life I have greater access to the loving and humorous parts of myself and can therefore tolerate even the more negative parts. Breast cancer has become only a piece of the quilt that is my life. I needed to be finished with it, to put a border around the experience. Inside that border are patterns that are familiar to my life, some interesting, some less appealing, and all the flaws that contributed to the creation of the piece. In looking at the piece as a part of the whole quilt, I can view it from different angles, in different light, in relation to all the other pieces.

My present task is to take this broader view, to regain a sense of the fullness of my life. My family helps me with this: they insist that I wasn't only angry when I was sick. David remembers vividly how demanding, unkind, and impossible I was, but, he jokes, even in healthy times I've been known to be difficult. He often reassures me that in the worst of moments I still managed to be loving to the children. Zach and Molly are rather matter-of-fact about the experience. They remember that I cried a lot and went to bed early, but cancer was simply part of their short lives. What else did they know? They had not lived long enough to realize that ordinary life is different from their experience in the past few years. I am their mother now, and I was their mother then, even with cancer. They loved me as I flailed about, trying not to drown, though they undoubtedly wished I'd learned to swim better.

The hard task for all of us is to integrate each of our experiences of cancer into who we are. I catch glimpses in David, Zach, and Molly, not to speak of myself, of the ways in which each of us has internalized some traumatic aspect of the experience, hardly modified by time.

For David, there is depression. Before my breast cancer, he had not known the feeling of waking up and dreading the day. Nor had he known the kind of anger he felt toward me during my illness. Now that these emotions are familiar to him they can easily be reawakened. Fortunately, he retains his sense of humor. He now jokes that, if I die, the next woman he dates will need to present a complete set of CAT scans first. I can't blame him.

He has a shorter fuse now and loses perspective more easily, perhaps because, like me, he lives with the knowledge of illness and death as ever present possibilities. One evening in the week preceding my last CAT scan, he came home looking haggard and worried. When I asked what was wrong he listed the college's budget crisis, a looming deadline for his manuscript, a delay on the subway, and a mistake that the bank made in our account. I pointed out that not everything is a cancer diagnosis. Our experience, when we can call on it, does highlight the insignificance of many of life's problems.

And what is the legacy of my cancer experience for my children? When I allude to how upset and unavailable to them I was during my treatments, Zach and Molly look at me as if they don't have the faintest idea what I mean. Most likely they're not aware of the painful ways in which the experience affected them or they're aware only in ways that are, at their ages, inexpressible.

Zach coped with my illness by insisting, perhaps desperately, that everything would be fine, that I would get better and life would return to normal. He continues to cope in this way—maintaining that there are no problems, that he's not upset, downplaying the threat that cancer poses to his mother and to himself. One evening a while ago, I came through the door, cheerful but tired. Zach heard me sigh and said to me matter-of-factly, "Yeah, some days are hard: work, lymphoma, making dinner." He acknowledged the fact of cancer in my life, in our life, but he let me know by his tone that he wanted to keep the discussion light.

Because he has rarely spoken of this cancer experience, I wonder what he acknowledges to himself about it. When he learned that his friend's father had committed suicide,

Zach was stunned and shocked and without a way to cope. He wanted to lie down on our bed but needed our help to walk there. He kept saying that he wanted to put this out of his mind, but he couldn't. When we talked with him about our friend's depression, he made a connection to me and my depression when sick. He let me hold him and asked me over and over, "You're not depressed now, are you, Mom?" He, like David, tends to keep his feelings private, and only rarely do we get a glimpse of his worry. Most of the time he works hard in school, is busy with friends, talks on the phone behind closed doors.

Molly is different. The mountains and valleys of her emotional life form a landscape that we can view daily. She is always forthright: she wants my hair to grow longer; asks why my one breast is harder than the other; complains that I won't carry her book bag and violin as I did before I became protective of my arm.

She has always been intense, and for the most part her intensity serves her well: she is passionate about life— about learning, friendships, music. Her forthrightness and sense of outrage bode well for her future strength as a woman. But since my illness she possesses an intense rage. When tired and frustrated, she becomes a living embodiment of my more desperate moments during treatment; her anger escalates quickly into a fury that echoes my own. It's uncanny to hear how she took in my rage, which must have sounded terrifying to her, and made it part of herself. When she expresses her anger toward me, she feels guilty at the thought that she's hurt me, fearful that I am fragile as I was during my cancer. I am stronger now, but she still fears hurting me.

For me, there is still the profound terror I felt then in the middle of the night, when I awakened from dreams about dying and stared into the darkness. If I no longer cohabit with this fear, it remains frighteningly close to the surface, ready to emerge at the slightest provocation, whether it be speaking to my sister about her precarious health or simply feeling my lymph nodes and imagining them slightly swollen. Sometimes I feel momentarily afraid in just leaving the house, as if any change will be accompanied by a catastrophe.

My friend Laurie died last year. I miss her. The other women I described in the book have recovered, each in her own way living with the threat of a recurrence and the wounds left by her breast cancer. I imagine that these women feel a deeper sadness than they knew before, as I do. For me, that pain was expressed in wrenching sobs when I was sick. I've always been able to express my most painful and unnameable feelings through tears, but then my sobbing took on a different quality. It seemed meant neither to bring me comfort nor to be heard by anyone. It gave voice to the utterly inconsolable loneliness that I felt. I cry like that rarely now, only when fearful of serious illness in myself or people I love. But the background music of my life is more somber. I know how easily life can slip away, and the possibility of death is no longer remote. Ordinary life will never again be free of this awareness.

Perhaps for this reason I still keep myself at a slight distance from David, Zach, and Molly, sometimes refraining from expressing my love because to do so seems to bring pain along with it, a reminder of how afraid I am of losing them or of their losing me. This is the worst legacy of my illness—that I sometimes avoid knowing how deeply attached I am to them.

So each of us carries the experience of cancer into our lives; some feelings rest more easily in us than others. The cancer caused real emotional damage, and each of us lives with that damage, much as I live with my lost breast, my less flexible arm, my scars. We cope well and not so well at the same time.

I still think of those scenes in nineteenth-century novels where the mother is dying in an upstairs bedroom. The doctor stops by and the loving family hovers at the bedside day and night. In my fantasy, the mother faces death calmly in the comfort of that love. Or does she?

I've always wondered what it was actually like for the woman in the bed. Was anyone really with her in her dying? Did she feel held in her family's love or totally alone, isolated in her own closed circle? Probably there were moments of each; moments alone, in fear or acceptance, and moments together. I wonder how I would face death if I knew it was really happening. I imagine that sometimes I would be strong and loving, sometimes terrified and furious. Why should the last days of my life, or anyone's, be different from the rest? I've heard that one's consciousness shuts down before one's body dies. I like that idea. It's nice to know that, when the mother in the bed finally faces her death, she may experience it and be protected from it at the same time.

Acknowledgments

In writing this book I have had the privilege of working with three superb editors. Peter Dimock and Tom Engelhardt, both friends, graciously agreed to give me an honest appraisal of an early draft of my manuscript, a task that I imagine they approached with great trepidation. Peter convinced me that I had a worthy book, and suggested that I had organized it around the notion of ordinary life. The chance to share in Peter's excitement about the process of writing has been one of the great joys of this project. Tom provided unflagging support and invaluable advice at every point along the road to publication. Most importantly, he pushed me to remain true to the fierceness of my experience, and to avoid writing a different story than the one I had lived. Jonathan Cobb, my editor at W. H. Freeman, worked with me in a thoroughly collaborative way. Throughout the process of bringing this book to completion, he remained astute in his comments and attentive to nuance, always available, and genuinely respectful of me and of my book. To each of them I offer my deepest thanks for their expertise, and even more for their friendship.

This manuscript would never have reached these editors were it not for an appreciative early reading by David Rosner. Although at first I pretended to dismiss his enthusiasm as that of someone reading a book in which he is the hero, he gave me the encouragement I needed to proceed. As in every other aspect of our life together, he was generous, loving, and helpful.

Jerry Markowitz also read the manuscript early on and reminded me, periodically and insistently, of his belief in its value. Betsy Blackmar, Bill Leach, Dinitia Smith, Nancy Sprince, and Craig Zwerling provided me with very helpful suggestions on my first draft. A number of other readers offered useful comments along the way Alex Baker, Sara Bershtel, Jenny Brier, Pamela Brier, Blanche Cook, Ann Eisenstein, Bonnie Gitlin, Shelley Henderson, Martha Katz, Laura Kogel, Arlene Litwack, Adrienne Markowitz, Dennis Marnon, Elli and Robbie Meeropol, Sheila Rothman, Cindy Steiner, Andrea Vasquez, Patricia Van der Leun, Marilyn Williams, and Lee Zevy.

Arnhild Buckhurst typed an early part of my nearly indecipherable manuscript while Ines Dominguez typed the bulk of it, patiently adding round after round of changes. In gratitude to them I have learned to compose on the computer. The copyeditor, Patty Zimmerman, the proofreader, Eleanor Wedge, and the staff for my book at W. H. Freeman—Kate Ahr, Sheila Anderson, Susan Cory, Maia Holden, Blake Logan, Laura Spagnoli, and June Yoshii—have been professional and supportive in their dealings with me, making the preparation for publication not a frustrating experience but a gratifying one. *Dr. Susan Love's Breast Book* provided me with the information I needed to fill in gaps in my understanding. Anne Moore and Chip Cody graciously agreed to check my manuscript for factual errors. I am thankful to them for this, but even more for the genuine humanity with which they helped me through my breast cancer treatments.

My parents, John and Joan Conway, have provided me with unquestioning love and support, however far from home and remote from their experience I have roamed. It deeply saddens me that my father, who passed on to me his passion for reading and supported my first literary efforts, did not live to see the publication of this book. Sophie and Alex Rosner have loved me as a daughter and shared with me their astonishing energy for family, politics, work, and this book.

The many acts of kindness on the part of my extended family and friends during my breast cancer are underrepresented in these pages, although I carry with me vivid memories of their love and generosity. I am grateful to them and to my patients, who were willing to face with me the limits of my dependability and the threat to our relationship. I also owe many thanks to those women with breast cancer who shared with me their individual stories.

Finally, I wish to thank Molly and Zach for their exuberance, honesty, and humor. The image of their bright, open faces sustained me through many a medical procedure, and their compassion during my illness was astonishing. They have made my life infinitely richer and I am indescribably proud of who they are becoming. To them, and to David, I dedicate this book.

Kathlyn Conway
New York
July 1996